Ed Sullivan and Johnny Carson: The Lives and Legacies of America's Most Famous Late Night Talk Show Hosts

By Charles River Editors

Ed Sullivan in 1955

About Charles River Editors

Charles River Editors is a boutique digital publishing company, specializing in bringing history back to life with educational and engaging books on a wide range of topics. Keep up to date with our new and free offerings with this 5 second sign up on our weekly mailing list, and visit Our Kindle Author Page to see other recently published Kindle titles.

We make these books for you and always want to know our readers' opinions, so we encourage you to leave reviews and look forward to publishing new and exciting titles each week.

Introduction

Ed Sullivan (1901-1974)

"Open big, have a good comedy act, put in something for children and keep the show clean. I believe in getting the best acts I can, introducing them quickly, and getting off." – Ed Sullivan's explanation for the success of *The Ed Sullivan Show*

"Ed Sullivan will be around as long as someone else has talent." – Fred Allen

From the day television existed as an entertainment medium, giant companies have battled each other for viewers, but in the history of television programming, no show was as consistently excellent in the ratings as *The Ed Sullivan Show*, a variety show that brought on all kinds of acts, from dancers to artists and singers. It was the longest running show to maintain one time slot, and today it is widely remembered for introducing the nation to the likes of Elvis Presley and The Beatles. When Elvis was on the show in 1956, over 82% of the nation's entire television audience tuned in, a rating that would make even the Super Bowl blush. Indeed, being booked on *The Ed Sullivan Show* became so important for performers that Aretha Franklin once noted, "And I was booked once to go on 'Ed Sullivan' and I got bumped and ran out the back door crying."

The Ed Sullivan Show has been commemorated as one of the most influential programs in the history of American television, and behind it all was the seemingly unassuming man whose name was on it. Even after Ed Sullivan had become an American institution on the strength of his show, one critic from *Time* asked, "What exactly is Ed Sullivan's talent?" Or as comedian (and frequent guest) Alan King put it, "Ed does nothing, but he does it better than anyone else in television." Of course, Ed Sullivan did have plenty of talent, especially when it came to identifying others', and over the course of nearly two decades, he became America's biggest starmaker. While Elvis and The Beatles are most remembered, Sullivan helped open the door to Motown acts, and his show was so culturally significant that Reverend Al Sharpton said of those performances, "I grew up in the 1950s and '60s, when it was almost a holiday when a black act would go on Ed Sullivan."

Perhaps the most ironic aspect of Sullivan's fame is that almost everyone tended to agree that he was stilted and unnatural in front of cameras. In 1955, one writer for *Time* colorfully described Sullivan as "a cigar-store Indian, the Cardiff Giant and a stone-faced monument just off the boat from Easter Island. He moves like a sleepwalker; his smile is that of a man sucking a lemon; his speech is frequently lost in a thicket of syntax; his eyes pop from their sockets or sink so deep in their bags that they seem to be peering up at the camera from the bottom of twin wells." At the same time, however, the writer conceded, "Yet, instead of frightening children, Ed Sullivan charms the whole family."

To a degree, that may have worked in Sullivan's favor, because it allowed him to come across like an everyday American, even as he was introducing audiences to potential stars with talents that most could not hope to emulate. Of course, at the same time, all the attention paid to his show and its impact on Americana has helped obscure the man behind it all.

Johnny Carson (1925-2005)

"I know a man who gave up smoking, drinking, sex, and rich food. He was healthy right up to the day he killed himself." – Johnny Carson

Among America's comedians, few if any have had the kind of influence on pop culture and society like Johnny Carson, the iconic host of *The Tonight Show* from 1962-1992. In addition to winning too many awards to count, Carson is proof that imitation is the sincerest form of flattery, as admitted by subsequent comedy show hosts like Jay Leno and David Letterman, who not only vied to replace Carson but also used his format for their own shows (and still continue to do so).

Carson may have pioneered the format of *The Tonight Show*, but he had already been involved in comedy for decades before then, starting with performances as "The Great Carsoni" when he was still a teen. The magic shows and comedy continued into college, where he had a running gag about interviewing pigeons on rooftops and asking them about a local political controversy. Carson's work was hailed by comedians like Red Skelton, who invited him to become a writer for him, and Jack Benny, who invited him onto the show, all before he had turned 30.

For several years during the 1950s, Carson rotated around various daytime shows as host, meeting important friends like Ed McMahon along the way, but he made it big when he replaced

Jack Paar as host of *The Tonight Show* in 1962. For the next 30 years, his mix of monologues, skits, and interviews would make his show must-see television on weekday nights, turning him into the highest paid television personality of the 1970s, and giving him the creative freedom to bring others along with him. In addition to bringing along his sidekick McMahon, Carson let guests host the show occasionally as well, thereby giving the spotlight to comedians like George Carlin, Letterman, Leno, and Joan Rivers. On the 25th anniversary of his debut on *The Tonight Show*, Carson earned a Peabody Award that labeled him "an American institution, a household word, the most widely quoted American."

Ed Sullivan and Johnny Carson: The Lives and Legacies of America's Most Famous Late Night Talk Show Hosts examines the lives and careers of two of America's most important entertainment icons. Along with pictures of important people, places, and events, you will learn about Ed Sullivan and Johnny Carson like never before.

Ed Sullivan and Johnny Carson: The Lives and Legacies of America's Most Famous Late Night Talk Show Hosts

About Charles River Editors

Introduction

Ed Sullivan

   Chapter 1: Edward Vincent Sullivan

   Chapter 2: Eddie Sullivan

   Chapter 3: Ed Sullivan's Sport Whirl

   Chapter 4: Ed Sullivan Sees Broadway

   Chapter 5: Mr. Broadway

   Chapter 6: Sullivan in War and Peace

   Chapter 7: Toast of the Town

   Chapter 8: The Ed Sullivan Show

Johnny Carson

   Chapter 1: The Great Carsoni

   Chapter 2: Who Do You Trust?

   Chapter 3: The Tonight Show

   Chapter 4: Staying On Top of Late Night Television

   Chapter 5: Retirement

   Chapter 6: Good Night

   Online Resources

   Bibliography

Free Books by Charles River Editors

Discounted Books by Charles River Editors

Ed Sullivan

Chapter 1: Edward Vincent Sullivan

"My father was, in every sense, the head of the family but my mother was its heart." – Ed Sullivan

On September 28, 1901, twin boys were born into the Sullivan home in New York City. Their father, Peter, was a man already hardened by the disappointments of life; he had come to New York City from his family's farm in upstate New York to take a good job as a city clerk, but instead, he found that it was a land of hard work, where the best job that he could get to support his growing family was as a milkman. Thus, Peter had to get up before dawn and drive a wagon through the dirty, smelly streets of turn-of-the-century Harlem. Their mother Elizabeth, on the other hand, refused to let her circumstances shape the way she viewed life and remained determined to make the best of things.

One of the twins, Danny, was sickly and could not seem to gain weight, eventually dying at just 10 months old. He would be joined much too soon by the Sullivan's next child, Lizzie, who died at 20 months. However, the other twin, Edward Vincent, was as healthy as his brother was frail. He was little brother to Helen and Charles, and he would become the older brother of other children, but not until his mother put her optimistic but determined foot down. She insisted the family would have to move out of Harlem and into a healthier place.

Though Peter initially thought this would be impossible, Elizabeth would have her way, so in 1906, the family moved to Port Chester, a sleepy, old fashioned town about 25 miles from the city. Peter found work at a hardware factory, while Lizzie kept herself busy having and raising their children. She could be stern when needed, but her natural outlook on life was light and gentle, and there was more music in the Sullivan home than there was shouting.

Meanwhile, young Ed never met a sport he didn't like, and whether he was at school or in a nearby field, he could always be found playing something. He earned some cash caddying at the nearby golf course, but baseball in particular helped shape his life view when he found himself playing against a good African-American team. Professional sports were decades away from being integrated, but small, local teams played against anyone they could find, and Sullivan would later note, "When we went up into Connecticut we ran into teams that had Negro players. In those days this was accepted as commonplace, and so my instinctive antagonism years later to the idea that a Negro wasn't a worthy opponent or was an inferior person."

Perhaps because of his interest in sports, Sullivan was not a good student at St. Mary's Parochial School, often failing to live up to the straight A standard set by his older sister Helen. The only subject he had any interest in was English, and he read vociferously through all the great classics of the era. Given that, it comes as little surprise that Sullivan sought to take advantage of the United States' entry into World War I, dropping out of school and getting a job at a local defense plant. He worked long enough to save money for a train ticket to Chicago, but his plan to enlist in the army fell through because he was only 16 years old.

After finding himself homeless in the Windy City, he got a job at a freight yard, but the stress of living on his own finally proved too much for the teenager, so he returned home and to high school. However, during his senior year, Ed Sullivan began writing the sports section of the school newspaper, which opened up a whole new horizon for him and led to a job with the *Port Chester Daily Item*. While working for the paper Sullivan covered everything from weddings to wrestling matches and fires to funerals. He also worked in the printing department and once recalled, "I've never worked so hard before or since." Of course, he preferred writing about sports to all other assignments, which inevitably led to controversy whenever some of his readers considered his comments, especially those related to his high school team, biased.

Though hardly the valedictorian, Sullivan was nonetheless invited to make a speech during the commencement exercises, and a local paper reported, "He delivered his address with a natural ease that served to make his words all the more impressive and called for extended applause when he had finished." That was certainly one of the last times anybody said Sullivan demonstrated "natural ease" on stage.

After he turned 19, Sullivan left Port Chester and moved to Connecticut to take a position as a sportswriter for *The Hartford Post*, but before he could even write a single article, the paper was sold and he was fired. Though he had never worked for the paper, he still received two weeks' salary as part of his severance pay, so he decided to remain in Hartford until he could figure out something else to do. Fortunately, an old friend helped him find new work at the *New York Evening Mail*. He started there in January 1920, covering local high school and college games.

Chapter 2: Eddie Sullivan

"If you do a good job for others, you heal yourself at the same time, because a dose of joy is a spiritual cure. It transcends all barriers." – Ed Sullivan

Sullivan had long wanted to return to life in the big city, and now that he had the chance, he relished his new home and developed a new style of writing to go with it. While his voice in Port Chester had been friendly and folksy, in New York his writing became sharper, and many of his barbs were aimed at the wealthy. He found this new style served him well. And like many young men his age, when not cover sporting events, he frequented New York's various nightclubs, some of which were seedy. In fact, it was at one of these, the "Silver Slipper", that he had his first brush with organized crime. The old-time gangsters took a liking to the young man, putting him in some very interesting positions. He would later tell the following story: "Fay had just bought the 'Rendezvous' from Marleau and Duffy and apparently he hadn't paid up…. Marlow said to him, 'Just a reminder, Larry, I've got to get money that by Monday or you'll find your ears lopped off.' That's how friendly I was with those guys. I got to overhear a conversation like that. I remember that line about lopping off ears…"

From a professional standpoint, the highlight of Sullivan's reporting career came when he got to interview boxing legend Joe Dempsey. He would later recall, "When I knocked at Dempsey's door, he opened it himself – and I remember how big he was. He seemed to fill the doorway. He was wearing a loud striped bathrobe and he was smiling." The two men soon established a pleasant rapport and remained friends for years.

Dempsey

Weeks after his 22nd birthday, Sullivan joined the *New York Leader* as sports editor, and this paper was a long way from the *Port Chester Daily Item* in both geography and politics. Where the *Daily Item* prided itself on its moral, conservative Republican tone, the *Leader* existed primarily to promote the Socialist Party in America. Sullivan, who would later be seen as both the ultimate right-wing prude and also the man that introduced America to Elvis and the Beatles, had no problem making the transition. To him, it was all about the sports, but even in the sports world he found plenty of things with a political nature to write about, including the following:

"Yesterday's near-riot in Columbus, Georgia, precipitated by the Mike McTigue – Young Stripling championship fight, can be traced directly to the Ku Klux clan [sic.]. McTigue, an Irish Catholic, managed by Joe Jacobs, a Jew, has as much chance of getting an even break in Georgia as the well-known snowball has of enduring the scorching blasts of Dante's Inferno."

When the *Leader* closed down after only six weeks production, Sullivan traveled south to Ormond Beach, Florida, where he got a job as an event planner and publicist for a local golf course. The skills he mastered there would later come in handy as he coordinated stars for his famous show, but even though he enjoyed the warm winter weather during his few months in the Sunshine State, Sullivan missed the excitement of New York and jumped at the chance to move back north. Once back in the city, he moved from one job to another until he finally landed a job with the *New York Evening Graphic* in late 1924. Though this paper was really nothing more than a tabloid in the great tradition of yellow journalism, it did give Sullivan a chance to meet his first true love.

Her name was Sybil Bauer, and Sullivan met her while he was covering a swim meet in 1925. Bauer was an Olympic Gold Medalist in swimming and had broken a number of world records in the backstroke. When the two met, it seemed to be love at first sight, and Bauer was the first woman that Sullivan ever "took home to mother". Such was his affection for Bauer that he broke his long-standing policy of avoiding Port Chester in order to take her there and introduce her to his family.

Sybil Bauer

When they met, Bauer was 21 years old, and though not beautiful in the classic sense, she nonetheless possessed a sort of girl next door prettiness, along with a swimmer's lean figure. The only problem was she lived in Chicago, so to make the long distance relationship work, Sybil would come to the East Coast for occasional swim meets and Sullivan would take the train to Chicago every chance he got. Before long, it was obvious that the two were seriously interested in each other.

Tragically, fate intervened in early 1926 when Bauer was diagnosed with advanced stage cancer. With very few treatments available at that time, the malignancy soon spread throughout her body. Once the poster child for good health, she was soon bedridden. Though Sullivan maintained contact with Sybil, he also began to look around for another girl, especially after he was told that Bauer would not be recovering. Thus, even as Bauer was in her dying days, Sullivan was already dating a girl named Sylvia Weinstein. Though it may seem in hindsight that Sullivan was behaving poorly, he was still very young and clearly coming to grips with suffering the first major loss of someone he loved.

When Sybil entered the hospital for the last time in November 1926, Sullivan left New York with a diamond engagement ring in his pocket and proposed to her at the hospital. She accepted, and the two announced their engagement to the papers. How much either of them knew about the future is open to speculation, but given that she died on January 31, 1927, it seems likely that they both knew there would never actually be a wedding. Sullivan had returned to New York after they became engaged, but he hurried back to Chicago when he heard the end was near, and he was by her bed holding her hand when she died. After the funeral, Sullivan returned to New York with the diamond ring in his pocket, and when he was later asked to describe her on the occasion of her induction into the Swimming Hall of Fame in 1967, Sullivan wrote simply, "Sybil, a girl from Chicago, was a very attractive girl. Most of us sportscasters had a crush on her. I know I did."

Chapter 3: Ed Sullivan's Sport Whirl

"Walter, what can I do with a cringing coward like you? If I hit you, you might get hurt. If I spit in your eye, it will be coming down to your level." – Ed Sullivan

Once back in New York, Sullivan continued his on-again, off-again relationship with Sylvia Weinstein, but while the two were obviously enamored of each other, they also faced what seemed to be insurmountable obstacles. The most worrisome one for both of them was the problem of their respective religions. Sullivan, while not particularly devout, was still a good Catholic boy from a good Catholic family, and Weinstein was a nice Jewish girl from a nice Jewish family. Sylvia's family was more flexible, but Ed's parents were strongly opposed to their son marrying a Jewish girl. This led Sullivan to frequently break off seeing her, only to call her a few days later and say that they should get back together.

Ed and Sylvia

In spite of his love and his inability to live without her, Sullivan still appeared to have no interest in marrying Sylvia, but things changed in the spring of 1930 when Sylvia informed Sullivan that she was pregnant. They decided to get married at City Hall and then have their marriage blessed that evening at the local Catholic Church. Sylvia agreed to Sullivan's request that their children be raised in his faith, so with that, on April 28, 1930 Ed Sullivan and Sylvia Weinstein were married. They then called their respective parents and told them the happy news. While Sylvia's parents' good-naturedly accepted their daughters surprise marriage, the Sullivan's were horrified, and it would take Sylvia several years to win them over. She eventually did so, and it was a big help when she gave birth to a daughter on December 22 and named her Elizabeth after Ed's mother.

At this time, Sullivan was still working for the *New York Evening Graphic*. While the majority of this paper's stories were written to appeal to the most prurient of his reader's interests, Sullivan wrote for a higher purpose. He had his fair share of gory details about boxing matches, and he was willing to report when a major sports star was caught not living up to the country's most wholesome values, but Sullivan also used his column, "Ed Sullivan's Sport Whirl", to promote a subject that he felt passionately about: the rights of African-Americans in sports and all other parts of American life. For instance, not only did he interview and cover African-American fighters, he also shared their concerns about their personal safety, quoting boxer George Godfrey, "I saw pictures of colored man strung up to posts after the Johnson – Jeffries fight....I resolved that I would never try that again....[My promoter] believes that the country has grown more tolerant, but he refuses to believe that our present degree of tolerance can prevail against the passions which are a great deal older in any of the present generation."

It seems that the match between the *Graphic*'s love for controversy and Sullivan's desire to promote fairer treatment for African-Americans was a match made in heaven. It did not hurt that Sullivan also had a way with people. Brian Mallen, one of the editors at the *Graphic*, remembered, "While his associates ran hither and thither in a rush of activity, Sullivan just lounged around and talked to people. He got more use out of the chair than anyone connected with the place….His friendly person's attribute of easily making acquaintances gradually spread his personality around New York. Those who mistook his easy-going gait as an indication of languor, however, were wrong. It was purely a matter of mathematics. It would take him half the time to write his stories that others needed. The reason was that he never had to stop to find the right word, an angle, a good start, or to look things up. They cascaded freely right into his typewriter, attesting to an uncanny gift of expression and memory."

It was also while working at the *Graphic* that Sullivan met Walter Winchell. Like Sullivan, Winchell was just getting his start in his field, but the main difference was that while Sullivan would eventually make his name by promoting stars, Winchell would make his by tearing them apart and becoming the ultimate gossip columnist. Their relationship through the years would be best described by one biographer as a "feud – friendship." While the two seemed to be always bickering, there were also times when they found that the things that they had in common drew them together into something like a friendship.

Winchell

Though Sullivan managed to maintain an amicable enough relationship with Winchell, he was not able to resolve his differences with everyone who crossed him. For instance, when Dan Parker made some snide remarks about him in the *Daily Mirror*, Sullivan slapped him with a lawsuit for $200,000 for libel and defamation of character. Though the court ultimately decided in his favor, Sullivan would later say, "I settled with the Hearst lawyers for my lawyers' fees, about $850, I think. They were astonished when I said I didn't want any money for myself."

Sullivan would soon find himself better understanding the world in which both Parker and Winchell wrote. The collapse of the stock exchange and the economic depression that it caused made it hard times for newspapers by 1931, and as the *Graphic* cut back on its staff, the thing the tabloid editors knew would sell was Broadway gossip. They decided that Sullivan should be their new gossip columnist, and in his farewell column, Sullivan's predecessor made the following friendly welcome to the man who was replacing him:

> "I understand Eddie's going to use his picture in this column. It's a grand idea, because this Sullivan fellow is one of the good-looking, he-man type of fellas. When he turns his firm chin at a certain angle, he is a dead ringer Gary Cooper.

Running his picture should help him a lot in the matter of mail from gal readers, and mail's mighty important to a columnist. It's only fair to warn Eddie, of course, that his home life is a thing of the past. He'll be coming home anywhere from 5 to 8 in the morning. He'll be coming home worn out, tired, grouchy and resentful at the world in general. He'll toss around in bed wondering what in the world use for a column the next day."

For their part, the *Graphic* went all out to promote Sullivan's new column, including a half-page ad complete with a headshot of Sullivan in a jaunty fedora and the following announcement: "He's a curiosity! He actually was born and brought up along the main stem of the town. He is the pal of Jimmy Walker, Jack Dempsey, Marilyn Miller, Buddy Rogers, …, Gene Tunney, Paul Whiteman, Flo Ziegfeld, Babe Ruth - of Mrs. O'Grady and Officer 666 – and he will tell you all about them as you've never been told before. He's been famous as a reporter and sports reporter these many years. Maybe you know Ed Sullivan, but, if you don't, be sure to meet him Monday in the New York Evening Graphic."

Chapter 4: Ed Sullivan Sees Broadway

Ed Sullivan Sees Broadway made its first appearance in the Evening Graphic on July 1, 1931, and Sullivan wrote about how he viewed his job:

"So many have asked me my sensations in turning from sports to Broadway that I will answer them in this introductory column. I feel, frankly, that I have entered the field of writing which offers scant competition, a field of writing which ranks so low that it is difficult to distinguish any one columnist from his road companies….I've charged the Broadway columnist with defaming the street." – Ed Sullivan

The uppermost stratum of Broadway, as revealed in the writings of its contemporary historians, the columnists, is peopled with mobsters, cheap little racketeers and a vast army of phonies….As I sat at the gala opening of Hollywood Gardens on Friday night, I marveled to myself….I marveled at the phonies who were there for no better reason then they had a mad desire to be seen….I pledge you huge army of phonies will receive no comfort in this space. To get into this particular column will be a badge of merit and citation.

Divorce like this will not be propagated in this column….I will always experience greater pleasure in seeing Gus Edwards roughhousing with his wife then in seeing a celebrity flaunting his mistress.….So with high resolve and no fears, I enter upon my career as a Broadway columnist….I confess that the prospect of competing against the present field leaves me quite cold….It looks like a breeze and, as Mike Casale would say, 'weather clear, fast track.'"

Though he would later insist that he had not wanted to take the job, he nonetheless threw himself into the work with all the gusto he had previously given to sports writing. In spite of the blatant hostility with which he began his column, or perhaps because of it, he was an instant hit. In fact, *Variety*, the celebrity magazine, ran his first column in its entirety, adding, "Sullivan is well known, if not famous, as a sports reporter. He will become equally so as a Broadway writer if he continues the way he started. The tabloids have been called the trade papers of the racketeers. Sullivan is on a tab. His initial outburst sounds as if he intends to disprove the allegation. It's a great opening."

When Walter Winchell questioned Sullivan about his sincerity, Sullivan first vacillated, saying that he was just trying to get off to an exciting start, but when Winchell replied that he would accept that excuse as an apology, it led Sullivan to attack him physically. According to Sullivan's own testimony later, "I got so mad I grabbed him by the knot in his neck tie and pulled him over the table, right on top of the cheesecake. 'Apologize to you?' I said, '… I did mean it you and if you say one more word about it I'll take you downstairs and stick your head in the toilet bowl.'"

However, Sullivan did almost immediately give up on his plan to maintain the high road in his column; the very next week, he reported on his old friend Jack Dempsey's divorce, including the effect the legal fees were having on the man's bank account, saying, "the ex-champion is seriously considering a fight at Reno against a guaranteed tanker. Dempsey would promote it, and would not have to cut Estelle in on the debt." When Dempsey contacted him expressing his shock at reading the story, Sullivan added insult to injury by printing Dempsey's telegram in his next column.

Though they disliked him, the stars of Broadway also feared Sullivan and soon began to pander to him. As a result, he found himself more popular with rising stars than he ever had been before, and perhaps not surprisingly, he loved it, as he admitted in one of his columns, "So many have asked my reaction to the new field of work that I will tell them now that Broadway columning is more varied and more interesting then sports columning. I believe that the people you meet in theater and its wings are, in the aggregate, smarter and more interesting."

Nevertheless, even if he enjoyed his work, Sullivan was still unhappy with his personal life, and his dissatisfaction with what he was doing came to a head on his 30th birthday. Sylvia would later recall that it was "one of the unhappiest days of Ed's life. I'll never forget that day as long as I live. There he was looking as if the end of the world had come. And he felt he was getting old and not getting where he wanted to be. He didn't have national prominence – and that's what he wanted. I was perfectly happy with him the way he was but he was born with a desire for big success."

Things only seemed to be getting worse in July 1932 when the *Graphic* shut down, but fortunately, Sullivan was quickly invited to bring his column over to the *New York Daily News*.

This proved to be a tremendous boost to his career, as the *Daily News* was a respectable paper with a solid and widespread following. Not only did the publication allow Sullivan to continue to report on the lives of the rich and famous, it also allowed him to take on a subject nearer and dearer to his heart: the plight of the working man in Depression era America. While Sullivan continued to report on who was seeing who, he also used his column as an opportunity to chastise the wealthy for taking advantage of those less fortunate.

Though Sullivan was at heart a populist, he still enjoyed rubbing elbows with the elite and spending his evenings hopping from one nightclub to another. A reporter who was sent to follow him around one evening wrote, "He seldom gets home before 5 AM, in the meanwhile having taken in, on a typical night, '21,' the Stork Club, the Hollywood, Dave's blue Room,….Courvoisier brandy is his only but not single drink; then it's bed until one or two in the afternoon. The column is written – at home. That takes a couple of hours and Sullivan then drives down to the Daily News, reads his mail, and waits while the composing room gives him a proof." Sullivan also reviewed new Broadway shows, though he was more inclined to release one-liners about the productions than to offer serious criticism.

Needless to say, this lifestyle left little time for a normal home life, but Sylvia did not mind either. She enjoyed going out to dinner with Ed much more than staying home by the fire, and the two had enough money to hire a good nanny for their daughter Betty. Thus, while they were enjoying caviar and cocktails in a New York nightspots, young Betty was just as happy over a bowl of macaroni and cheese at a local diner. Though this might strike modern parents as odd or even cruel, Betty never complained either in youth or adulthood, and she always remained close to both of her parents.

Chapter 5: Mr. Broadway

"Don't place too great an emphasis on defeat, and don't yield to the American habit of overemphasizing victory, because one is no more important than the other. Through life, you'll encounter your share of both of them, and you'll find that defeats are really the prep school of victory." – Ed Sullivan

Still determined to be a national sensation, Sullivan attempted to create his own opportunity. In 1933, he wrote a script for a movie called *Mr. Broadway*, and casting himself as the star, he conceived it in two parts. The first part would consist of footage of him visiting one New York hotspot after another, stopping at tables to chat with celebrities and generally being himself. The second part would be a fictional melodrama. Using his Broadway connections, he raised enough money and attracted enough stars to make the movie, and among those making appearances were Jack Benny and Jack Dempsey (who had apparently forgiven Sullivan for his columns). Making the movie more than just a "Who's Who on Broadway", Sullivan also took time during the film to express the desperation of those who would never see their names in lights. This allowed him to segue into a dark melodrama of a love triangle surrounding a pilfered necklace. Edgar G.

Ulmer, who Sullivan had to direct, later complained that he "didn't like it at all, because Sullivan forced it into one of these moonlight-and-pretzel things. It was a nightmare, a mixture of all kinds of styles."

Though the critics agreed with Palmer, Sullivan remained undeterred, and the following year he released *Ed Sullivan's Headliners* (1934). It wasn't liked any more than his initial attempt. Of course, Sullivan had plenty to fall back on, because the paper had promoted him again, and he was now writing five columns a week. This allowed him to go toe-to-toe in competition with his old friend Walter Winchell, who had already taken over the Stork Club as his main headquarters. Instead of going around town looking for celebrities to interview, Winchell simply remained at the club and waited for celebrities needing attention to come to him. Sullivan decided to do the same thing, letting word get out that he would be hanging around the El Morocco nightclub each night and was willing to receive anyone who wanted to stop by his table. His strategy worked, and in the end his popularity not only exceeded Winchell's but outlasted it too.

Sullivan was popular in New York, but he would still spend the next decade trying to break into the big leagues. After once more attempting to launch a radio show, he tried his hand on Broadway, acting as the Master of Ceremonies for a vaudevillian production called *Ed Sullivan's Dawn Patrol*. It opened in 1935 to positive reviews and made good money over the next few years, but it still didn't lead to his major goal of national fame.

His next big shot at that came when Fox Movietone News hired him in April 1936 to narrate the newsreels that were so popular in America. Sullivan decided to parlay this opportunity into a chance to become a Hollywood columnist and persuaded the *Daily News* to reassign him from New York to Hollywood. The little Sullivan family was soon living in a quaint California bungalow in Tinsel Town, and Sullivan was spending his days going from studio to studio chatting with actors and actresses ranging from Shirley Temple to Joan Crawford, as well as producers directors, cameramen, and anyone else that would give him the time of day.

At first, Sylvia found it difficult to adjust to the slower pace and more suburban feel of 1930s Hollywood. New York was a big city with bright lights and glitter, while Hollywood at this time was more of a bedroom community where people with small families gathered together in the evenings for drinks and conversation in each other's homes. But as time went by, they made more friends and the Sullivan's were soon enjoying jumping from party to party as much as they had from club to club.

In addition to the romantic intrigues surrounding America's Hollywood idols, Sullivan also wrote about the wheelings and dealings that these stars endured in the business. Of course, the biggest excitement to hit Hollywood prior to World War II was the making of *Gone with the Wind*, and Sullivan was there, following and reporting on every twist and turn, from the search for a Scarlett to the hirings and firings of one director after another, and eventually the movie's release.

Unfortunately, Sullivan had one serious character flaw that would always cause him problems in life, especially in his chosen industry: he was overly sensitive. When it came to rumors, mocking, and teasing, he could dish it out but not take it. In 1938, he, along with the other important Hollywood columnists, were invited to review 11 films being released that year, but of the 11, the only one Sullivan really liked was *Alexander's Ragtime Band*. Though the public would agree with him, the other critics thought his comments naïve and said so. While a more self-confident columnist might have taken their comments in stride, Sullivan was offended and would continue to gripe about his ill-treatment for months to come.

By this time, Sullivan decided to try his hand at moviemaking again. He released *There Goes My Heart*, a romantic comedy that opened it to mildly interested reviews, but it suffered from criticism that it was too much like *It Happened One Night* to be considered original. After that, Sullivan was still able to convince Universal Studios to make his next film, *Big Town Czar*, and he also persuaded them to cast him in one of the roles, but it was panned by both the critics and the audiences. So was his next picture, *Ma, He's Making Eyes at Me*, which opened in 1940.

All the while, Sullivan's columns continued to be among the most popular in the nation, and over the last few years of the 1930s, he interviewed everyone from Katherine Hepburn to Walt Disney to W.C. Fields. However, his continual engaging in and failure at moviemaking was becoming an embarrassment for the *Daily News*, since it was paying his salary after all. They insisted that he returned to New York and his work on Broadway, and after some complaining and blustering, he finally complied.

Chapter 6: Sullivan in War and Peace

"Patronize the standard clubs and restaurants; avoid the down-at-the-heels clip joints...Avoid the jackals who will offer to guide you to disreputable joints, where they will drug your drinks and swipe you bankroll and perhaps hit you on the head…it's a great street, and we want you to enjoy it." – Ed Sullivan

When Sullivan returned to New York, he found a city that was in as much of a funk as he was. New York in July 1940 was experiencing one of the worst heat waves in its history, and the Sullivan family was depressed over having to leave the more moderate California temperatures. Sylvia missed the friends that they had made in California, not to mention the more reasonable hours Ed had worked, and Betty missed their house with a lawn because Ed insisted that they live in an apartment close to Broadway. Of course, Sullivan himself missed his involvement with Hollywood stars.

Still looking to make his mark in the entertainment world, Sullivan staged yet another failed Broadway production in January 1941, after which he turned his eye to radio. He hosted another radio show through the summer, but he and his audience remained in a sort of sluggish doldrums until the Japanese attack on Pearl Harbor woke them and the entire country up. Suddenly, people were feeling alive again; there was plenty of work to do and not enough hands to do it. Everyone was busy, and night clubs opened up again, offering whiskey and dancing to young man in uniform about to ship out overseas. The entire country threw itself into the war effort, and the patriotic Ed Sullivan was no different. In addition to volunteering as a Civil Defense warden, he put together yet another show to entertain those needing a break from the day's headlines. Entitled the *Harlem Cavalcade*, it featured an all African-American cast performing classic vaudevillian routines. It was a success, and Sullivan seemed to finally have what he wanted in life.

Ironically, Sullivan was too busy with his war work to bask in the glow of *Cavalcade's* success. Drawing on the skills he had learned through years of entertainment, he organized war bond rallies, hospital benefits, and special shows for servicemen. Though he was often criticized for promoting his own importance in his columns, Sullivan's work during the war did bring comfort to many families, and perhaps the most famous of his wartime columns concerned a young man from Georgia named Arthur Ford. If Sullivan is to be believed, he spent a good bit of time with Ford, entertaining him and arranging for visits from celebrities he wanted to meet before the young man died. Sullivan wrote about Ford's last days and then concluded his article with this heartfelt remarks for his parents: "[I]n his last struggle, they should know that their son, or brother, was not a small-town Georgia boy alone in a big city of Yankees… He was with people who considered him one of their own, and when he died, in the north, of wounds received while landing on a faraway shore, we regretted it bitterly, while acknowledging that the wearied and wounded boy finally had found one opiate to ease his pain."

While Sullivan undoubtedly cared about the soldiers he encountered, he was still obsessed with building his career, and as a result, he jumped at the chance to launch Ed Sullivan Entertains, a live radio broadcast from Club 21 in New York, in 1943. Unfortunately, Sullivan seemingly worked too hard to make the show a success, because his interactions with his guests seemed over-rehearsed and fake. As a result, the show never made it big and was eventually canceled in June 1944.

Throughout the war years, Sullivan and all other respectable columnists in the nation had downplayed their writings about scandal and underhanded behavior among celebrities. The feeling was that the nation needed to pull together, and that unity was more important than pointing fingers. However, with the end of the war came a sort of readjustment, as columnists tried to find out what their writing would look like in postwar America. For his part, Sullivan chose to turn his attention more towards political scandals than those surrounding the entertainment industry, a turn he began by accusing the city's police force of being on the take.

By the time the war ended in 1945, Sullivan had all but accidentally transformed himself from a Broadway columnist into the most popular MC in New York. His work at bond rallies and other fundraisers had sharpened his repartee and made him every organization's top choice to host an event, so for the next several years, he would spend any time that he had left over after writing his column hosting one production after another. Whether he knew it or not, this type of volunteer work would actually be the thing that opened the door to national stardom.

It began with a request from the heart fund drive that he host 30 short radio shows to promote the drive. Sullivan agreed, and he worked with Marlo Lewis to put together an amazing lineup of talent, including Bob Hope, Jack Benny, Jerry Lewis, and Bing Crosby. This series was a success, and 1948 proved to be a banner year for fundraising for the drive. It also caught the attention of the new CBS television network, which recruited Sullivan to host a weekly variety show originally called *Toast of the Town*.

Chapter 7: Toast of the Town

"Television is sight and sound, similar to the movies but dissimilar in that there are no retakes. What happens at any exact moment on a television stage is written in indelible ink, and not one tear can remove any part of it…" – Ed Sullivan

Though it was destined to set all sorts of television records under a different name, *Toast of the Town* did not get off to a better start more than any of Sullivan's earlier efforts in entertainment. When it was first broadcast in June 1948 from CBS Studio 50 on Broadway, critics panned both Sullivan and the show, with one particularly caustic reviewer observing, "He got where he is not by having a personality, but by having no personality." In fact, Sullivan's television mannerisms were so stiff that some people who watched his show thought he had Bell's Palsy, a condition that prevents sufferers from moving their limbs with any fluidity.

However, what Sullivan did have that most of his contemporaries lacked was connections. He knew everyone who was anyone on Broadway and in Hollywood, and he was able to recruit these people through a friendly combination of gentle persuasion and veiled threats to appear on his show. Moreover, Sullivan's stiffness on camera may have been his greatest strength, because it prevented him from focusing the show on himself and ensured the focus would be on the guests. Sullivan's awkwardness also gave the impression that he was not a seasoned performer out to show off but just a regular guy introducing audiences to celebrities they had always dreamed of meeting. The result was an ever stronger combination of guest acts that attracted more and more attention from viewers. As comedian Fred Allen would later say, "Ed Sullivan will last as long as someone else has talent."

One of the celebrities who often appeared on Sullivan's show, comedian Alan King, once said "Ed does nothing, but he does it better than anyone else in television." In some ways, what he said was true, because on the air, Sullivan seemed to do almost nothing. However, off the air he was a man driven to find the very best for his program. Years of living in the center of the entertainment industry had given him a sense of what people wanted, and he was determined that they should have it.

The end result was a show that appealed to people of all ages and backgrounds. Each episode would include some sort of act, from vaudeville to magic shows. There would also be a comedian or two doing standup, as well as a popular singer, and for those who had a more highbrow taste, Sullivan would often interview a guest from the Broadway stage. To appeal to young audience members, the puppet Topo Gigio, a mouse from Italy, would pop-up to put on a short show. If any athlete was making major headlines, chances are he or she would also be making an appearance on Sullivan's show.

Time magazine summed up, in a strange way, Sullivan's show in 1955 when it said that Sullivan was "a cigar-store Indian, the Cardiff Giant and a stone-faced monument just off the boat from Easter Island. He moves like a sleepwalker; his smile is that of a man sucking a lemon; his speech is frequently lost in a thicket of syntax; his eyes pop from their sockets or sink so deep in their bags that they seem to be peering up at the camera from the bottom of twin wells. Yet, instead of frightening children, Ed Sullivan charms the whole family."

One thing that being on television frequently did for Sullivan was that it helped thicken his previously thin skin. His demeanor and mannerisms were so unique that they cried out for imitation, and fortunately, when men like Rich Little and Frank Gorshen began to imitate him, Sullivan took their gentle barbs with good grace and laughed along with the audience. Johnny Carson also did a pretty good Sullivan impersonation, and even Joan Rivers had the way that he stood down pat. However, it was Will Jordan who proved to be the man most capable of capturing both Sullivan's look and mannerisms. When Hollywood wanted someone to portray Sullivan on screen, they turned to Will Jordan, who appeared as Sullivan in six separate pictures, including *I Wanna Hold Your Hand* and *The Buddy Holly Story.*

Will Jordan

Another thing that that impersonators found it easy to pick up on was Sullivan's collection of catchphrases, including "for all you youngsters out there...", and "and right now, right here on our stage..." Of course, Sullivan's most famous catchphrase was his announcement each evening that tonight they had "a really big shew."

In addition to the catch phrases, Sullivan often stumbled over what he was saying and got words wrong, which provided some humor but also made him seem all the more average. In one famous case, he got the name of a musical category wrong when he told the audience, "Now ladies and gentlemen, as everyone know, whenever any new musical trend had evinced itself in the popular trends-the Charleston or the black bottom or any of the rhythm songs-the first area to find out about it in advance is Harlem. A couple of weeks ago I went up to Harlem, I'd seen these shots in the newsreel about thousands of people jamming the streets around the Apollo theater, all trying to get in to see Dr. Jive's rhythm and roll, rhythm and color, rhythm and blues. So here is Dr. Jive!"

During his lifetime, Sullivan's political affiliations vacillated between both the major parties, as well as between socialism and populism, but he always considered himself a loyal American first and foremost. Unfortunately, as the 1940s gave way to the 1950s, being a loyal American took on a whole new meaning. Thus, when Sullivan scheduled dancer Paul Draper to appear on his show in 1949, he drew the ire of Hester McCullough, a woman who had accused Draper of being a communist sympathizer. Ford Motor Company, Sullivan's sponsor, demanded that Draper not appear on the broadcast, but Sullivan stood his ground and Draper performed on Toast of the Town early in 1950.

What Sullivan did not realize was that McCullough had a strong and active following, so after the program aired, Ford was inundated with letters and telegrams demanding to know why they were sponsoring a "pinko". In order to save his show, Sullivan had to do something he hated more than anything else in the world: apologize. Not only did he have to write a letter of apology to Kenyon and Eckhardt, the advertising agency for Ford, but he also had to promise to never again schedule such a controversial figure on his show.

Still sympathetic to the civil rights cause, Sullivan also insisted on standing his ground when it came to having black performers on: "The most important thing [during the first ten years of the program] is that we've put on everything but bigotry. When the show first started in '48, I had a meeting with the sponsors. There were some Southern dealers present and they asked if I intended to put on Negroes. I said yes. They said I shouldn't, but I convinced them I wasn't going to change my mind. And you know something? We've gone over very well in the South. Never had a bit of trouble." Sullivan invited legendary African-American actor Paul Robeson to appear on his show not long after the Draper appearance. It is unclear whether or not he knew it at the time, but Robeson was at that time under investigation as a communist. Though the Robeson incident was not as serious as the one involving Draper, Sullivan was still concerned and decided to begin running anyone who would appear on his show past Theodore Kirkpatrick, editor of the anti-communist Counterattack newsletter. He would later confess in his daily column, "Kirkpatrick has sat in my living room on several occasions and listened attentively to performers eager to secure a certification of loyalty. On some occasions, after interviewing them, he had given them the green light; on other occasions, he had told them 'Veterans' organizations will insist on further proof.'"

Robeson

Chapter 8: The Ed Sullivan Show

"I grew up listening to the Beatles and being an ardent Beatles fan when I was in third grade all the way to adulthood, and listening to all kinds of music that came to us either at the flea market or in our living rooms or on the 'Ed Sullivan' show - all these places we were influenced by." – Sandra Cisneros

In 1955, CBS confirmed what everyone else in America already knew when they changed the name of *Talk of the Town* to *The Ed Sullivan Show*. After all, no one who ever appeared on the show could doubt for a minute that it was indeed Ed Sullivan's show, and some performers learned this the hard way. In November 1955, Bo Diddley was in New York to appear on Sullivan's show when the host himself requested that he perform "16 Tons", which had been made popular by Tennessee Ernie Ford. Diddley felt that this song would not be good for his career and instead sang his own big hit "Bo Diddley." He was never invited to appear on *The Ed Sullivan Show* again.

Picture of Bo Diddley by Masao Nakagami

To be fair, after the Draper incident, Sullivan was quite aware that not only could he censor, but he could also be censored. In 1956, he announced that Ingrid Bergman would appear on his show, the public outcry was loud because Bergman had scandalized the nation back in 1949 by having an affair with director Roberto Rossellini and having an illegitimate child with him. Bergman, along with Yule Brenner and Helen Hayes, were in Europe filming *Anastasia*, and since they could not come to him, Sullivan went to them and shot footage of interviews with each that he planned to air on his show. However, by the time he got back to America, it was clear that CBS was not going to allow him to embroil them in yet another controversy. Thus, Bergman's interview was cut from the production, and to justify that move, Sullivan tried to make the audience feel it was their choice: "Now I know that she's a controversial figure, so it's entirely up to you. If you want her on our show, I wish you'd drop me a note and let me now to that effect. And if you don't--if you think it shouldn't be done, you also let me know that, too. Because I say it's your decision and I'd like to get your verdict on it."

Knowing that he had to play by certain rules in order to survive in the business, Sullivan was very public with his concerns about Elvis Presley and the immoral behavior the young singer was reported to be promoting during his performances. As Elvis set out to promote his game-changing new album in 1956, he embarked on a series of high profile national television appearances, and though his performance on The Ed Sullivan Show would become historic in short time (remembered primarily for the scandal it created), it was actually preceded by another national television appearance equal in its scandalous content. In April and June, Elvis performed on the *Milton Berle Show* on NBC. The first program, shot onboard the USS Hancock was uneventful and received a raucous reception from on-deck and television audiences alike, but in the two-month interval between the NBC broadcasts, Elvis performed a two-week engagement in Las Vegas and undertook a mini-tour throughout the United States. During the tour, he heard Freddie Bell and Bellboys perform the blues song "Hound Dog," a Leiber and Stoller song that was a hit for Big Mama Thornton three years before Elvis discovered it. Elvis fell in love with the tune, asked permission to sing it and quickly made it the closing number in his acts, to great approval from his audiences.

The fervor that "Hound Dog" and his similar performances inspired among fans started to catch more attention that Elvis ever bargained for. During the springtime mini-tour, Elvis played a show in La Crosse, Wisconsin, where he was watched by his usual rapturous teen audience, as well as a federal agent reporting to none other than FBI Director J. Edgar Hoover. A report on the letterhead of the Catholic diocese's La Crosse newspaper sent directly to Hoover following Elvis' local show read, "Presley is a definite danger to the security of the United States... [His] actions and motions were such as to rouse the sexual passions of teenaged youth..." It went on to detail the "harm" Elvis caused by describing two girls who were elated to receive the star's autograph on their thighs and abdomen. TIME magazine took a far less accusatory, though no less bewildered, position on Elvis' onstage motions, writing of him, "In a pivoting stance, his hips swing sensuously from side to side and his entire body takes on a frantic quiver, as if he had swallowed a jackhammer."

When Elvis appeared for his second performance on Berle's show, he agreed to the host's request that he leave his guitar backstage during his performance, thus requiring him to dance as he sang. As he sang "Hound Dog" on NBC's Hollywood stage, he held the microphone stand in one hand and moved within the limited confines of center stage in punctuated moves that involved only minor swivels or thrusts. This scandalized many Americans, including Ed Sullivan, who said both publicly and privately that he would never invite Elvis on his show. However, by the fall of 1956 Elvis was simply too famous to ignore, especially after Sullivan got beat in the ratings by Steve Allen's show for the first time when Elvis went on it. Sullivan humorously sent Allen a note that read, "Steven Presley Allen, NBC TV, New York City. Stinker. Love and kisses. Ed Sullivan." But more importantly, Sullivan decided to have Elvis appear and offered him an unprecedented $50,000 for three shows.

When "Elvis the Pelvis" performed on NBC's *Steve Allen Show*, he had been forced to perform "Hound Dog" in white tie and tails directly into the face of a basset hound that was wearing a top hat. He later called it the most ridiculous thing he was ever made to do in his career, and it all but ensured his appearance on *The Ed Sullivan Show* would be different. Still, rumors abounded that Sullivan would attempt to control the performance; Sullivan was convinced that Presley employed some type of device to facilitate his gyrations and that he stuffed his trousers with a

Coca Cola bottle to heighten the effects. The host figured he could get around potential controversy by simply shooting Elvis from the chest up, thereby ensuring viewers didn't see his hips.

Ironically, when Elvis first appeared on *The Ed Sullivan Show* on September 9, 1956, his performance immediately made the episode one of the most famous television programs in history, and Sullivan himself was not there to see it. The previous month, Sullivan had been involved in a serious automobile accident in Connecticut that broke several bones and shattered some of his teeth, so he was still at home recovering from his injuries and so was not there to welcome the King of Rock 'n Roll. Instead, Charles Laughton introduced Presley and got all the attention surrounding the big performance.

Following his introduction, prior to singing his first song, "Don't Be Cruel," Elvis noted that being on the show was "probably the greatest honor I've ever had in my life," even after the guest host Laughton accidentally introduced him as "Elvin Presley." The episode had 60 million viewers, which was 82.6& of the American viewing audience. As of 2012, it stands as the single greatest share of the viewing audience watching the same program in television history. In time, it proved to be a breakthrough moment for Elvis, and the moment when he became a bona fide national icon.

Elvis performed for Sullivan's audience again in October 1956 and once more in January 1957, two days before his 22nd birthday. Following his final performance, Sullivan praised Elvis on-air, "I want to say to Elvis and the country that this is a real decent, fine boy, and wherever you go, Elvis, we want to say we've never had a pleasanter experience on our show with a big name than we had with you. So now let's have a tremendous hand for a very nice person!" Yet the third performance was a far cry from his Sullivan début or any of the programs that preceded it because Elvis dressed in costume and even sported eye makeup. It was also the only one of the three performances for which Sullivan actually honored the waist-up filming strategy he described when he first made the deal in September. It was a staid affair by comparison to the earlier shows due to the limited way in which he was filmed, but it was nevertheless a wild departure from earlier performances due to his costuming.

Of course, Elvis would not be the last rock 'n roll singer to aggravate Sullivan. When *Buddy Holly and the Crickets* appeared on his show in 1957, everything went well, but when Sullivan invited them back in January 1958, he requested that they not sing their current hit, "Oh, Boy!", because he felt that the song was too provocative. Holly replied that he had already promised his friends back in Texas that he would be singing the song in their honor, which only made Sullivan madder. Sullivan retaliated by calling the band to rehearse on very short notice, and when only Holly himself appeared, Sullivan quipped, "I guess The Crickets are not too excited to be on The *Ed Sullivan Show*." Holly retorted, "I hope they're damn more excited than I am." This response made Sullivan even angrier, and though he could not cut them from the program entirely, he determined that they would only be able to sing one song instead of the two previously planned.

When it came time to announce them, he deliberately mumbled Holly's name, making it sound something like "Buddy Hollett." Sullivan also instructed the sound man to turn off the microphone to Holly's electric guitar. Furious, Holly was determined to make the performance work, and he sang so loudly that he could still be heard in spite of the missing microphone. The fans went wild, and the episode was one of Sullivan's most popular, which all but forced him to invite Holly back for a third performance. By this time, however, Holly had had enough, and he was also so popular that he no longer needed Sullivan. He informed America's favorite host that there was not enough money to pay him to return to the show.

Buddy Holly

Of course, Sullivan got along quite well with many of his guests. In 1958, two Canadian comedians known as Wayne and Shuster made their first of 67 appearances on *The Ed Sullivan Show*, and that same year, Sullivan's own popularity reached a new high when he appeared in a comic rubber mask on the popular game show What's My Line? He also made a guest appearance on *Mr. Adams and Eve*, a popular CBS sitcom, and in 1961, he was invited to guest host the other American favorite, *The Red Skelton Show*. Sullivan not only hosted the episode but appeared in a number of the skits in Skelton's place, including a humorous portrayal of himself as "Eddie the freeloader." In 1963, Sullivan even finally made it into a major motion picture when he appeared as himself in the film *Bye-Bye Birdie*.

The 1960s were such a controversial time in American society that it would have been impossible for Sullivan to host a consistently up to date show and avoid all controversy. He found himself again in the center of conflict when he invited Bob Dylan to appear on the show in 1963. Dylan planned to perform his current hit, "Talkin' John Birch paranoid blues." Though Sullivan had approved the song, the network censors were concerned and insisted that Dylan not perform it. When Dylan walked out of dress rehearsal, Sullivan supported his decision not to perform.

By September 1963, Beatlemania was sweeping through mainland Europe, and after touring Sweden that October, the band returned to London Airport on October 31 to a large group of screaming fans who waited in the rain to see the band. The fans' display was so large it delayed the arrivals and departures of other airport patrons, including one notable traveler: Ed Sullivan. After Elvis, Sullivan was determined never to be scooped again, so when he noticed fans' responses to The Beatles, he was determined to have them on his show. He would later recall, "In late September 1963 when we were taping acts in London, I looked up the Beatles, sight unseen, because London papers gave tremendous Page 1 coverage to the fact that both the Queen's flight and the newly elected Prime Minister Douglas Home's plane to Scotland had been delayed in takeoffs for three hours. The reason: the airport runways had been completely engulfed by thousands of youngsters assembled at the airport to cheer the unknown Beatles!"

Sure enough, the scene Sullivan witnessed at the airport compelled him to take a meeting with the group's manager, Brian Epstein, in early November, during which time they negotiated a deal that would present the Beatles to the American public in February 1964. Brian leveraged the deal in a pitch to U.S. record label Capitol Records, which worked like a charm. Throughout November, Epstein carefully positioned all of the pieces necessary to début the band in the United States with a big promotional drive from an American record label paving their way. It was contrary to the band's hope to achieve a number one record in America before performing there, but the opportunities were too big not to seize. The band's rise to fame at home had been nothing short of meteoric. After little more than six months since the release of their first record, The Beatles were the best-selling musicians in British history. Epstein figured their success in Britain warranted a chance on America, and Sullivan was certain of their success. Days before the band was set to perform on his show, he joked with his audience, "Coincidentally, if anyone has a ticket for The Beatles on our show next Sunday, could I please borrow it? We need it very badly."

On February 7, 1964, the band boarded a plane in London to fly to New York for *The Ed Sullivan Show*. The scene at Heathrow Airport was so chaotic that lines of policemen had to link arms to blockade the crush of riotous fans. The band was certain they still had a long way to go to achieve a comparable level of fame in the United States, so they were shocked and thrilled when JFK Airport radioed the pilots mid-flight to say that there was a mass of fans waiting for them already. By the time they touched down just outside of New York City, 5,000 screaming fans had swarmed the airport. The Fab Four were photographed disembarking the plane and waving to fans from the tarmac.

The Beatles arrive in New York

The next day, the Beatles were scheduled to rehearse for the show, but George missed the practice time due to a severe bout of streptococcal tonsillitis and a 104-degree temperature. Meanwhile, the three healthy Beatles were at the Ed Sullivan Theater meeting their host. Sullivan acquired a prop Beatle wig that he playfully held on to as he met John, Paul and Ringo for a photo session. He joked that if George wasn't well enough for the show, he'd don the wig and take the stage himself. George was still sick when the band returned to practice in the morning on February 9, hours before the show, but he rallied for the live performance that night. About 30 minutes before the show began, the Beatles received a telegram from Elvis Presley and his manager Colonel Tom Parker, in which the King congratulated the band and wished them luck. Sullivan would read the telegram live to a captivated American audience, which ultimately totaled over 73 million. Nearly one in three Americans watched the Beatles on *The Ed Sullivan Show* that night, and Sullivan's introduction was among his most famous: "Now yesterday and today our theater's been jammed with newspapermen and hundreds of photographers from all over the nation and these veterans agree with me that the city had never witnessed the excitement stirred by these youngsters from Liverpool who call themselves the Beatles. Now tonight, you're going to twice be entertained by them-right now, and again in the second half of our show. Ladies and gentlemen...the Beatles! Let's bring 'em out!"

The Beatles then continued their stateside tour, but while in Miami, the band broadcast a second *Ed Sullivan* appearance on February 16, and Sullivan would later introduce them when they appeared in their famous Shea Stadium concert in 1965. The band would go on to appear a total of four times on Sullivan's show, and they would also film a number of special appearances to be played when they were not available to appear live.

   While Sullivan hit it off with The Beatles, he made an enemy of Jackie Mason in October 1964, or at least Mason made an enemy of him. While Mason was taping his monologue, Sullivan learned that the show was about to go to live because an address by President Lyndon Johnson had ended sooner than expected. Sullivan put up two fingers to let Mason know that he only had two minutes left and needed to wind up his monologue. The audience became distracted by Sullivan's gestures and stopped laughing at Mason's jokes, making it appear to those watching the show on television that the audience did not think Mason was very funny. Mason, in hopes of getting the audience's attention again, cried out, "I'm getting two fingers here! Here's a finger for you!" While he is unclear whether or not Mason actually extended his middle finger in Sullivan's direction, Sullivan certainly thought that he did and became furious. Mason was banned for the show for a year and a half before he was allowed to return. By that time the issue had been resolved, but the legend of the finger remains.

   By this time, CBS was showing the programs in color, but while it was performed live on the East Coast, the West had to accept a taped version. This meant that future generations would be able to enjoy the show in reruns and also on DVD. However while they saw the Byrds perform in December 1965, no one knew at the time that lead singer David Crosby had such an argument with the director that the band was banned from the show. The following year, The Doors were also banned after they refused to change the lyric, "girl, we couldn't get much higher" from their hit song "Light my Fire". CBS believed that the line could be misinterpreted to advocate drug use, but The Doors, despite promising to make the change backstage, went ahead and sang the song as written. As that episode indicated, and perhaps not surprisingly, Sullivan was still struggling to keep up with the contemporary trends set by his performers; before they had gone on stage, Sullivan had told Jim Morrison, "You boys look great, you ought to smile a little more." And when the show's producers informed The Doors they'd never be invited back again, Morrison replied, "Hey, man, we just did the Sullivan show!"

Morrison

In January 1967, Mick Jagger took a more pragmatic approach. When Sullivan told The Rolling Stones to change the lyric "let's spend the night together" to "let's spend some time together" Jagger went along with it. However, he got away with displaying his ire by rolling his eyes and making faces whenever he sang the words. When the band's manager contacted Sullivan about having the group perform a second time, Sullivan replied, "Before even discussing the possibility of a contract, I would like to learn from you, whether your young men have reformed in the matter of dress and shampoo."

By this time, Sullivan made hosting the show look so easy that *Time* magazine asked the question, "What exactly is Ed Sullivan's talent?" The point they missed, of course, was that Sullivan's talent was in finding, meeting, and managing people, and he was so good at it that he made it look easy. While the shows that were controversial and ended with some sort of hard feelings are easily noticed and pointed to, it is important to remember that a huge majority of the episodes that he put on live each week went off without a hitch. That is no small feat for anyone, but an even bigger one for a "square" middle-aged man to pull off during the rock 'n roll revolution.

Part of what made *The Ed Sullivan Show* unique in its time was that Sullivan insisted that most of his performers perform live, singing directly into the microphone rather than lip-synching a previously recorded performance. At the same time, he knew that it was not always possible to have this level of production. For example, recently issued DVDs revealed that B. J. Thomas lip-synched "Raindrops Keep Falling on my Head" in 1969. The obvious reason for this is that he was performing under a sprinkle of real water and therefore could not use a microphone to make his voice heard.

Another factor that made *The Ed Sullivan Show* unique and garnered respect for Sullivan from the younger generation was his support of African-American performers. As has been mentioned before, Sullivan had always fought for equality between the races and refused all efforts to keep his television show segregated. So, when the Jackson Five single "I want you back" gained Billboard's top spot, Sullivan not only had them on his show but footed the bill himself. After the Jackson Five's first appearance, Sullivan noted of Michael Jackson, "The little fella in front is incredible."

Likewise, he supported The Supremes by having them appear on his show 17 times. Though Diana Ross would later complain that he could never remember their names, his support opened the door for their success and that of other Motown groups, including The Temptations and The Four Tops. Sullivan never forgot old friends either; when the dancer Bill "Bojangles" Robinson, died, Sullivan used his own money to provide the American legend with a proper funeral.

Still a populist at heart, Sullivan made sure that music popular among working-class Americans had a prominent place on his show. Thus, *The Ed Sullivan Show* became one of the first variety shows to invite country performers to appear. Soon word got around that big names in Nashville were just as welcome on his show as big names in New York, and this opened the door for another group of often ignored performers. This eventually led to the production of Hee Haw, as well as giving country singers like Glen Campbell a chance to host their own television shows.

Throughout his life, Sullivan had been notorious for his poor memory, but by the beginning of the 1970s, he was having so many problems remembering names and faces that some celebrities speculated that he might have had Alzheimer's disease. When Paul McCartney ran into him, Sullivan did not recognize him, and he wasn't even able to make the connection after McCartney introduced himself. Even when he explained that he was a member of The Beatles, Sullivan remained confused and simply smiled and nodded.

By this time, *The Ed Sullivan Show* itself was on its last legs. While he had for decades been able to keep up with the taste in music of the American public, he was now 70 years old and tired of the rat race of making a weekly show. While it was no doubt discussed that perhaps someone else could take his place, the heads at CBS knew better: there would not be another Ed Sullivan. Even still, when they finally canceled the show in 1971, Sullivan was so shocked and furious that he refused to appear on the final episode. Was this rage itself another symptom of Alzheimer's? It is hard to say, because Sullivan had a hot temper all his life, and age had done nothing to improve it. After tempers cooled, he was willing to remain with the network and even hosted the show's 25th anniversary special in 1973.

Had Sullivan lived, he might have indeed eventually been diagnosed with the dreaded disease, but he would not live long enough. Instead, he was diagnosed in September 1974 with end-stage cancer of the esophagus. When doctors told his family that he had very little time left, they decided to keep the news from him and instead let him believe that the pain he was feeling was merely a symptom of his ulcer acting up again. Sullivan died five weeks later on October 13, 1974, in New York. At the funeral, held at New York's famous St. Patrick's Cathedral, over 3,000 people braved the cold rainy day to pay their final respects to the man. Following the funeral mass, Sullivan's body was interred at the Ferncliff Cemetery in Hartsdale New York.

Johnny Carson

Chapter 1: The Great Carsoni

"I was so naive as a kid I used to sneak behind the barn and do nothing." – Johnny Carson

John William Carson was born on October 23, 1925 into an All-American kind of family in Corning, Iowa. His father, Kit Carson (no relation to the famous cowboy), worked at the local power company, while his mother, Ruth, stayed home raising Johnny, his older brother Dick, and his younger sister Catherine. The Carson's moved several times during Johnny's early years before settling in Norfolk, Nebraska in 1933, and though America was in the throes of the Great Depression at the time, the Carson's did not feel the pinch as much as most families. Kit never lost his job, so even though they weren't wealthy, they also didn't have to wonder where their next meal was coming from.

That security ensured young Johnny had a normal childhood, and as a child, Johnny Carson was an unusual mixture of shy wallflower and class clown. However, the older he got, the more he enjoyed losing himself in another personality or in a performance, and he explained how he became comfortable making that kind of personality transition: "That's one of the things that goes against the grain of being brought up that you should be modest; you should be humble, you shouldn't draw attention to yourself. Well, to be an entertainer you gotta be a little gutsy, a little egotistical, so you have to pull back sometimes when people say, 'Well, he's stuck-up.' Stuck-up is only another word for self-conscious. You aren't stuck-up. You are aloof because you aren't very comfortable so you put up this barrier." He also noted, "There comes a time or a moment when you know in which direction you're going to go. I know it happened to me when I was quite young. I think it's when you find out that you can get in front of an audience and be in control. I think that probably happened in grade school, 5th or 6th grade, where I could get attention by being different, by getting up in front of an audience or even a groups of kids and calling the attention to myself by what I did or said or how I acted. And I said, 'Hey, I like that feeling.'"

When he was 12, Johnny's friend Phil McNeely showed him a catalog for magic tricks, and Johnny was fascinated, later recalling, "It showed exactly how [to do tricks] with a kit of stuff from some mail order magic house in Chicago. So I sent for it. I started making the things I needed and it was fascinating. I spent hours at it. Magic became my all-consuming interest." With magic, Johnny found a new way to relate to the world, and in time, it would give him both a social and financial future. His parents, however, thought it was merely a passing fancy, but while it was going on, his mother figured she should indulge him a little, so that Christmas, she gave him a beautiful black velvet banner embroidered with his new stage name: "The Great Carsoni".

From that time on, Johnny would perform for anyone he could get to watch. For a penny or two, any child in the neighborhood could be treated to the amazing feats of magic performed by their young neighbor, and as he got better, he added small parties and church socials to his venues. Carson would later recall, "I can't say I ever wanted to become an entertainer, I already was one, sort of—around our house, at school, doing my magic tricks, throwing my voice and doing the Popeye impersonations. People thought I was funny; so I kind of took entertaining for granted…. It was inevitable that I'd start giving little performances."

For young John Carson, performing helped him navigate the frightening waters of adolescence. He would remember his time in high school fondly, saying, "When I was a kid, I was shy. And I think I did that because it was a device to get attention. And to get that reaction is a strange feeling. It is a high that I don't think you can get from drugs. I don't think you could get it from anything else. The mind starts to do things that you didn't even realize it could do. I suppose it's the manipulation. I suppose it's the sense of power, the center of attention and the me-ism. And performers have to have that."

By the time Johnny was a senior in high school, his reputation for humor won him a place on his high school yearbook committee. As class historian, he took it upon himself to write a very humorous "last will and testament" for his high school's yearbook, the Milestone: "I, John Carson, being of sound mind and body (this statement is likely to be challenged by my draft board and the high school faculty)…can visualize 20 years from now when you sit by the radio (listening to Roosevelt)…you will say to your son—"I wish I could get hold of that #?$))&/ Milestone Staff."

Even at this young age, Carson displayed several hints of the style of humor that he would later make a part of America's late night experience. First, there was his self-deprecation, and Carson would build his career on the back of his own flaws. Also, there is the reference to Franklin Roosevelt, who was by this time well into his third term, a subject of both amusement and consternation for many in the nation. Finally, Carson pushed the envelope of what was then considered good taste with his discreetly veiled "profanity."

However, for Carson and most of his classmates, adolescence ended abruptly, because many high school graduates immediately had to enter the military. In fact, the thought was always with them, as Carson's reference to his draft board indicates. On June 8, 1943, just days after he graduated from high school, Carson entered officer training at Columbia University, and he later transferred to Millsaps College, where he continued to practice his magic tricks between drilling and learning how to shoot. By the time he received his commission as an ensign, the war was almost over, but he was still sent to the Pacific theater and assigned to the USS *Pennsylvania*. His initial work provided a rude awakening for the 19 year old, because a few weeks before he arrived, the *Pennsylvania* had been hit by a Japanese torpedo. According to Carson, "It practically blew off the stern and killed twenty guys. So she headed into dry dock at Guam. I was assigned to damage control, I guess maybe because I was the youngest officer and the most recently arrived. And my first assignment was to go down into that hole in the stern and supervise the bringing out of those twenty corpses and their personal effects. Jesus, that was an awful experience. They'd been down there eighteen days by that time, and I want to tell you, it was a terrible job."

Carson in the Navy

To keep fit and blow off some steam, Carson did some boxing while in the Navy, during which he had a perfect 10-0 record, quite a feat for someone who had never boxed before. However, he did not have long to pursue either his boxing or his naval career, because the atomic bombings of Hiroshima and Nagasaki brought the war to an end only a few months after he was commissioned. During the time between the end of the war and his own decommissioning, Carson worked in communications and decoding, which gave him plenty of time to practice his magic and a unique opportunity to perform for a very special person. Once, while delivering a decoded message, Carson recalled, "I walked in with this thing, and there was [Secretary of the Navy] Forrestal with the admiral, having breakfast. He asked me my name, and if I planned to stay in the Navy. I said 'No, sir,' and he asked what I wanted to do after I got out of the service. Well, I hadn't really given it much thought myself, but I had to say something. So I said I'd always been interested in being a magician and entertainer. Forrestal said, 'Can you show us some tricks?' And the admiral pulled out a deck of cards from somewhere. And there I was, after being up all night, at six or seven in the morning on Guam, doing card tricks for the admiral and the Secretary of the Navy."

Secretary Forrestal

Once he was back at home, Carson returned to college and enrolled in the University of Nebraska, where he pledged Phi Gamma Delta and made extra money by performing his magic act for various campus and fraternity events. By this time, he was charging $25 a show, which was plenty of money to afford hamburgers and nice clothes. Committed to performing and comedy, he devoted his senior thesis to an in-depth examination of Jack Benny's style of humor, and this thesis, along with his class work, earned him a Bachelor of Arts degree in radio and speech in 1949. At his parents' insistence that he have something practical to fall back on, he minored in physics.

Jack Benny

Chapter 2: Who Do You Trust?

"Talent alone won't make you a success. Neither will being in the right place at the right time, unless you are ready. The most important question is: 'Are you ready?'" – Johnny Carson

As was typical in the 1940s, especially with young veterans, Carson married just a few months after he graduated from college. He had met Joan Wolcott on campus in 1948, and the two began dating. She later explained, "Johnny was vulnerable and boyish. He was shy, but he covered it up with a very superior, scornful air that I sort of saw through. There were all sorts of fellows around saying I love you, all this and that. But I fell in love with John, who didn't do any of that stuff. I fell in love with the man that he was. I believed in him." Johnny and Joan were married the following year, and Joan soon became pregnant, with their first son Christopher being born in the fall of 1950. He was quickly followed by Cory, and then Richard.

Meanwhile, Johnny had gotten his first job at WOW radio and television in Omaha. Unlike his idols, Jack Benny and Bob Hope, Carson did not cut his teeth in radio but instead jumped straight into the new medium of television. His first show was a morning program called *The Squirrel's Nest*. He would later recall, "The trick was just finding something to do. We had turtle races, one of the more exciting things. There was no money in television in those days but nobody cared because you were learning what it was all about. We were all caught up in the idea that we were on television. You'd just go in and they'd kind of roll a camera out and you were on the air."

By far, Carson's most famous bit surrounded a local political controversy. The Douglas County Courthouse in Omaha was infested with pigeons, and the city council was determined to get rid of them. Of course, some people felt that the birds were a charming addition to the building and should be left alone. For his part, Carson remembered, "I simply took the pigeon's side. And I did a remote broadcast one morning. I got up on top of the building with a microphone. And I said, 'Just get me a record with some coos that sound like doves of pigeons.' So I went up and I asked the pigeons how they felt about this attempt to remove them. And then I would play the cooing and I would interpret what they said, that they were very saddened at the fact that the city government would try to move them off a public building. It got a lot of press and finally I think the Natural Gas Building or something like that offered to take the pigeons."

Another routine that Carson enjoyed no doubt influenced the eventual development of "Carnac the Magnificent." At that time, studios would receive pre-recorded tapes of celebrities answering questions that deejays were then expected to ask on the air, but Carson thought it was fun to change the questions. For instance, he was supposed to ask singer Patti Page when she began singing, but instead, he asked her when she began drinking, making her taped reply more hilarious than accurate: "When I was six, I used to get up at church socials, and do it."

With his experience in Omaha under his belt, Carson was ready for something bigger, so in 1951, he packed up his growing family and took a "vacation" to California. However, what he was really doing was looking for a new job, which he found at KNXT, a Los Angeles television stationed owned by CBS. His show was called *Carson's Cellar* because he claimed it was the "bargain basement" of comedy, but his biggest problem was that he needed a sponsor. After wooing prospective companies for months, Carson finally persuaded American Home Products to come on board, but the maker of anti-perspirants and depilatories was not a good match for Carson's humor. By 1953, the show was off the air.

Fortunately, Carson soon had an offer from another source, because famous comedian Red

Skelton had seen *Carson's Cellar* and liked his style. He asked Carson write jokes and skits for his show. The following year, in 1954, Skelton was injured on the set and had to find a quick replacement to do the show that evening. He chose Carson, giving the young man his first national exposure. While this did not make an immediate difference in his career, it did plant seeds that would bear fruit well in the future, and Carson's name began to spread around the industry. One of the people that heard of Carson during this era was Jack Benny, who invited Carson to do a guest spot on his show. When Carson did a humorous job of imitating Benny and then claiming Benny was imitating him, Benny correctly predicted that Carson would soon find plenty of his own success as a comedian.

Red Skelton

Carson appearing on *The Jack Benny Show*

After Carson hosted a short lived game show called *Earn Your Vacation*, he had accrued enough name recognition that his next program was called *The Johnny Carson Show*. It premiered in 1955 and seemed destined for success, but the show was doomed to failure by an assortment of problems, as Carson remembered, "There were too many cooks telling me what to do and how to do it. There was no central control. The agency was putting people on without my knowledge, the scripts were being edited without telling me. I was sitting around like a dummy." As a result of these and other problems, the show only lasted just 39 weeks before being cancelled.

Disappointed with his time on the West Coast, Carson returned to New York City to look for more work, and he found it in 1957 as host of an afternoon game show called *Who Do You Trust?* The show had originally been called *Do Your Trust Your Wife?*, but the name was changed when Carson joined the show so that he could include unmarried guests. It was a big success, as each week featured new and well scripted interviews with average people from whom Carson would supposedly elicit surprising revelations. In many ways, it was one of the forerunners to the "reality shows" of the early 21st century, and it spawned similar gags with comedians interviewing people on the street, like Jay Leno's "Jaywalking" routine.

It is perhaps ironic that Carson was hosting a show about trust when he had so little of it in his personal life. By 1957, his marriage with Joan was on the rocks, but their marriage had always been plagued with problems from their earliest days. For one thing, the couple had radically different expectations about what married life should be like. Joan wanted a father at home each night, but while this was the image Johnny and Joan tried to portray to the public, especially during their many photo shoots for magazines, it was far from reality. In the real world, Carson believed that a man worked hard and long hours making a living, and that he was thus entitled to whatever type of fun he preferred, be it other women, drinking or just staying out all night with the guys. He did nothing to hide that he was often unfaithful from Joan; in fact, he was surprised that she even complained. When drunk enough and angry enough, he would lash out both verbally and physically, often leaving her with multiple bruises or a black eye.

For years, Joan kept their home life a secret, but the strain of living a lie began to take its toll, and she found herself needing someone to talk to. She began seeing a therapist and then other men. Perhaps she hoped that Carson himself would become jealous and that she would win him back, but he had little more interest in her fidelity than he did his own. He was fine with the status quo and didn't really care what she did, as long as she cared for the children and kept quiet about it. However, they couldn't go on as they were, and eventually, Joan insisted that Johnny move out in 1959. Carson would later say of the early days of their separation, "That's the lowest I've ever felt, the worst personal experience of my life. We'd been married ten years—since college, in fact. And children were involved—three sons. I think that's the worst guilt hang-up you can have, when children are involved. But divorce sometimes is the only answer. I think it's almost immoral to keep on with a marriage that's really bad. It just gets more and more rotten and vindictive, and everybody gets more and more hurt." Of course, that didn't stop him from cracking jokes about marriage, like, "Married men live longer than single men. But married men are a lot more willing to die." Or, "If variety is the spice of life, marriage is the big can of leftover Spam."

While Carson was losing one major relationship in his life, he was forming another. During his first year on *Who Do You Trust?*, he hired a new announcer named Ed McMahon, and McMahon quickly became the perfect match for Carson in both wit and quick thinking. Both men loved ad libbing, and McMahon proved to be one of the few that could keep up with Carson's sharp tongue. He was also satisfied with the number two slot and had no interest in trying to usurp his boss. Not only would McMahon become Carson's foil and business partner for the rest of his career, but he also became Carson's best friend. The two spent more time together off the set than they did on it, often finishing up their evenings in a nearby bar drinking into the early hours of the next morning.

McMahon

Unfortunately, while McMahon seemed to have a sense of self-control when it came to those late evenings, Carson was not as fortunate, and even he knew he had a problem. He would later recall, "We would go next door to Sardi's to have a small flagon of grape. And then we would come back to do a show at 6:30. And then we had one at 9:30 at night and I can remember coming in completely bagged. I'm not a good drinker, you know, two or three and I go bananas."

Indeed, before long, Carson's heavy drinking was affecting his performance on air, and his friends were concerned. They figured that since he was drinking more after his marriage ended, a new woman might help him cut back, and as a result, someone introduced him to Joanne Copeland. She worked at the studio as the hostess on *Video Village*, another afternoon game show they sponsored, but because living together would have caused too much scandal since Johnny was still technically married, Carson rented an apartment in her building the following year. They went places together and even took vacations with other couples, but they also argued and fought more than most couples. Still, they kept making up, even as Carson kept climbing the entertainment ladder.

Johnny and Joanne

Chapter 3: The Tonight Show

"New York is an exciting town where something is happening all the time, most unsolved." – Johnny Carson

In 1954, while Carson was writing for Red Skelton, comedian Steve Allen began hosting a late night program called *The Tonight Show*, and he all but created the genre of late night television, working without a script, hosting special guests and pulling crazy stunts as the situation demanded. Two years later, he left the show for something earlier in the evening, and Jack Paar took over for him. Paar was as high strung as Allen was relaxed, and soon Americans were making sure to watch the show every night just to see what was going to happen next.

By 1962, Paar was exhausted and ready to retire, and Carson was determined to replace him, even though he admittedly had little contact with Paar: "The only thing I can clearly remember…is that I met Jack in his office and said, 'Hi Jack!' I thought it was a very clever line. After all, I didn't want to overpower him. Beyond that I've had no dealings with him. I've never seen Jack Paar socially any place, and I was never a guest on the show when he was presiding. He might be an interesting guy to know. I just don't know. I really don't have the slightest idea what he's like."

Paar

Regardless, replacing Paar would make Carson the lord of the longest slot in television, almost

2 hours of air time every evening, but when he finally made his first appearance on the show, he opened to lackluster reviews. *The New York Herald Tribune* complained, "There was none of the free-wheeling frivolity, the titillating suggestive humor, the strong commentary, the boisterous what'll-he-do-next quality that so often sparked Paar's show. He is not the showman his predecessor was. But perhaps he will come along." Another critic, Jack Gould, was more optimistic, saying, "Mr. Carson's style is his own. He had the proverbial engaging smile and the quick mind essential to sustaining and season a marathon of banter…He began in an atmosphere mercifully free of impending crisis." The problem, of course, was that Carson had some huge shoes to fill. Jack Paar was an American institution, and even Carson's own mother was not sure he could do it, telling one reporter, "I thought it was interesting. I wasn't sure that John was the type for it. When Jack Paar had the show, it was more like an arena—so much controversy, all the time. John is a gentle, kind person. He's not controversial. But I think maybe he'll do all right."

Of course, the only people who really mattered were the viewing public, and they seemed more than ready to give Carson a chance. He carried around half of the viewing audience every night during his early months with the show, and those who tuned in watched with fascination as Carson introduced his own style to the show. For one thing, he used written scripts, right in front of him on his desk, rather than cue cards. While he had read and approved every word on them, the audience didn't know that, so if a joke didn't go over well, he tossed the paper aside as if he was just as surprised and disappointed as they were. This bit of farce gave him a credibility with his viewers and made them like him even better. Moreover, as viewers got to know him, Carson also got to know his audience, saying, "You have to tailor your material to the medium. I can look at a piece of material and know fairly well whether it will play and be amusing. You have to learn to be an editor. You experiment sometimes. I'm sure Mel Brooks is not a comic who reaches the great percentage of the audience. He's kind of wild—but when he's good, he's near genius. I'll put him on the show. I'm much better with a Sam Levenson. He talks about kids and schools, and he won't offend. You just have to rely on your own judgment. If you do make a mistake, you'll find out soon enough—because suddenly you won't have an audience."

Carson also had a definite goal in mind when he took over *The Tonight Show*, as he would later explain, "I wanted the show to make the most of being the last area of television that the medium originally was supposed to be - live, immediate entertainment. I decided the best thing I could do was forget trying to do a lot of pre-planning. It all boiled down to just going out there and being my natural self and seeing what would happen."

On the first night that the show aired, there was a musical theme in the background. Written by Paul Anka and called "Johnny's Theme," it would become as much a part of the show as the band and the bad jokes. It would go on to open every program through Carson's last night in 1992. Another way in which Carson made the show his own was by bringing in McMahon to be his sidekick. McMahon would later recall:

"My role on the show never was strictly defined. I did what had to be done when it had to be done. I was there when he needed me, and when he didn't I moved down the couch and kept quiet. ... I did the audience warm-up, I did commercials, for a brief period I co-hosted the first fifteen minutes of the show..., and I performed in many sketches. On our thirteenth-anniversary show Johnny and I were talking at his desk and he said, 'Thirteen years is a long time.' He paused long enough for me to recognize my cue, so I asked, 'How long is it?' 'That's why you're here,' he said, probably summing up my primary role on the show perfectly... I had to support him, I had to help him get to the punch line, but while doing it I had to make it look as if I wasn't doing anything at all. The better I did it, the less it appeared as if I was doing it....If I was going to play second fiddle, I wanted to be the Heifetz of second fiddlers....The most difficult thing for me to learn how to do was just sit there with my mouth closed. Many nights I'd be listening to Johnny and in my mind I'd reach the same ad lib just as he said it. I'd have to bite my tongue not to say it out loud. I had to make sure I wasn't too funny—although critics who saw some of my other performances will claim I needn't have worried. If I got too many laughs, I wasn't doing my job; my job was to be part of a team that generated the laughs."

Before long, McMahon's opening phrase, "Heeeeeere's Johnny", had become part of the American lexicon, and Carson's show was also legendary for his opening monologues, because he was so committed to spontaneity that nobody ever knew what he was going to say. He explained, "It's always been a ritual with me. I don't show it to Freddie or Ed or anybody. If you don't show it to anybody, then you get fresh reactions." Of course, this meant that the monologue might not garner the kind of reaction he hoped for, so he had a backup plan. If the monologue got no laughs, the band would start playing "Tea for Two", and Carson would dance until the audience loosened up. Thankfully, most of the monologues were popular, and they typically ended with Carson doing a clubless golf swing toward the orchestra. Guest hosts would start to mimic that signature move by pretending to roll bowling balls stage left in place of Carson's golf swing.

Carson with McMahon and bandleader Skitch Henderson on New Year's Eve 1962

During the summer of 1963, Carson surprised his friends, and even perhaps himself, by deciding to remarry. He arranged for Joan to fly to Mexico and quickly formalize their divorce, so that there would be as little attention called to the matter as possible. Then he and Joanne planned a small wedding for August 17. Still, even after he had a new wife, Carson's first love remained his show, and as he grew to love it more, so did the people in show business.

One of the things that Carson brought to his show was a cast of dozens, all played by him. For example, one of these characters was "Honest Bernie Schlock", the host of the "Tea Time Movie", who would come on with his "Matinee Lady" and try to sell the audience a very unusual and useless product during long breaks between short segments of the fictional movie. Over the years, Schlock would be "replaced" by Ralph Willie and then Art Fern.

Then there was Carnac the Magnificent, a turban wearing mystic who would always be introduced by McMahon in the same way and then trip over the step up to the desk in a bumbling fashion. On one occasion, the desk was set up so that Carnac could actually fall through it and break the desk after tripping over the step. After implying that Carnac had been involved in some recent national or international disaster, McMahon would announce, "I hold in my hand the envelopes. As a child of four can plainly see, these envelopes have been hermetically sealed. They've been kept in a #2 mayonnaise jar on Funk and Wagnall's porch since noon today. No one knows the contents of these envelopes, but you, in your borderline divine and mystical way, will ascertain the answers having never before seen the questions."

Carnac would hold the envelope up to his forehead, come up with an answer, and then open it up to reveal a question that made the answer humorous:

"Billy Graham, Virginia Graham, and Lester Maddox" ... "Name two Grahams and a Cracker!"

"Over 105 in Los Angeles" ... "Under the Reagan plan, how old do you have to be to collect Social Security?"

"V-8" ... "What kind of social disease can you get from an octopus?"

"Debate" ... "What do you use to catch de fish?"

"Baja" ... "What sound does a sheep make when it laughs?"'

"Sis boom bah."..."Describe the sound made when a sheep explodes."

Soon, being on *The Tonight Show Starring Johnny Carson* was a rite of passage for any aspiring star, a sign that someone had made it to the big leagues. Many of today's biggest names in show business made their first major network appearances on *The Tonight Show*, like David Letterman, who would go on to have his own show and be a major competitor of Carson's replacement, Jay Leno. Standup comedian Jeff Foxworthy first introduced the country to Rednecks on an episode of *The Tonight Show*, and many comedians who got their first big break on Carson's show, including Jerry Seinfeld, Ellen DeGeneres, Tim Allen, Roseanne Barr and Drew Carey, went on to become television stars in their own right and have situational comedies built around their routines. In many ways, Johnny Carson filled in the space left after *The Ed Sullivan Show* ended in 1971.

Though Carson could be nasty to his own writers and as difficult to please as possible, he was typically kind to newcomers. One of these, Joan Rivers, later remembered her first time on the show, "He understood everything. He wanted it to work. He knew how to go with me and feed me and knew how to wait….He never cut off a punch line and when it came, he broke up. It was like telling it to your father—and your father is laughing, leaning way back and laughing, and you know he is going to laugh at the next one. And he did and he did and he did....At the end of the show he was wiping his eyes. He said, right on the air, 'God, you're funny. You're going to be a star.'"

On the other hand, one thing Carson wouldn't do was assist an interviewee by engaging in mock laughter. Canadian comedian Mort Sahl remembered what happened if an interview wasn't going well, "The producer crouches just off camera and holds up a card that says, 'Go to commercial.' So Carson goes to a commercial and the whole team rushes up to his desk to discuss what had gone wrong, like a pit stop at Le Mans."

However, people were willing to take their chances because appearances on *The Tonight Show* were good for publicity and business. In early 1966, Milton Bradley released a new game called Twister, and though children found it somewhat fun, the product was not selling well and was in danger of being pulled from the market. However, when Carson played the human pretzel game on the air with bombshell Eva Gabor, sales went through the roof, and Twister has been an important part of American culture ever since.

For his part, Carson enjoyed his success and the money that came with it, but he was also aware that he owed something to the world that had been so good to him. His Midwestern background had instilled in him the importance of giving back, as he told one reporter, "It's silly to have as one's sole object in life just making money, accumulating wealth. I work because I enjoy what I'm doing, and the fact that I make money at it-- big money--is a fine-and-dandy side fact. Money gives me just one big thing that's really important, and that's the freedom of not having to worry about money. I'm concerned about values--moral, ethical, human values--my own, other people's, the country's, the world's values. Having money now gives me the freedom to worry about the things that really matter."

Chapter 4: Staying On Top of Late Night Television

"By the simple law of survival, Carson is the best. He enchants the invalids and the insomniacs as well as the people who have to get up at dawn. He is the Valium and the Nembutal of a nation. No matter what kind of dead-asses are on the show, he has to make them funny and exciting. He has to be their nurse and their surgeon. He has no conceit. He does his work and he comes prepared. If he's talking to an author, he has read the book. Even his rehearsed routines sound improvised. He's the cream of middle-class elegance, yet he's not a mannequin. He has captivated the American bourgeoisie without ever offending the highbrows, and he has never said anything that wasn't liberal or progressive. Every night, in front of millions of people, he has to do the salto mortale. What's more, he does it without a net. No rewrites. No retakes. The jokes must work tonight." - Billy Wilder, 1978

Early on, Carson developed a formula that would keep the show popular for decades; he would take off every Monday and have a guest host fill in for him. The first of these hosts, Joey Bishop, would appear on *The Tonight Show* more than 175 times, and along with movie star Jerry Lewis, he would be Carson's "go to" guest host during the 1960s. Though Carson respected and appreciated these men, and the others that would sub for him through the years, he was not intimidated by them or worried about his own standing: "The ratings always sag when there's a replacement for a time. I think I do a hell of a better show…but I think I do a better show because I have an affinity for editing and pacing. I make comedians look as good as I possibly can. This show is a combination of a lot of things—music, comedy, talk—but you must have a personality around which the show revolves. The show depends on how he works with the acts, the way he performs; his attitudes and opinions are what carries this kind of show."

While Carson was happy to take center stage and talk about someone else, he did not enjoy talking about himself, but as he became more popular, he was besieged by more and more reporters wanting interviews. To put them off, he created a list of answers that they could use to answer any of their questions.

"1. Yes, I did.

2. Not a bit of truth in that rumor.

3. Only twice in my life, both times on Saturday.

4. I can do either, but I prefer the first.

5. No. Kumquats.

6. I can't answer that question

7. Toads and tarantulas.

8. Turkestan, Denmark, Chile, and the Komandorskie Islands.

9. As often as possible, but I'm not very good at it yet. I need much more practice.

10. It happened to some old friends of mine, and it's a story I'll never forget."

While Carson was enjoying professional success, he was also happy on a personal level, as his second marriage seemed to be going well. He was under less pressure to succeed now, so he was able to spend his time as he liked instead of feeling like he had to see and be seen at all the best places. In talking about his evenings with Joanne, he told someone, "I don't like to go out much. We enjoy spending our time here, we have a comfortable home and we like each other's company. I'm not going to sit around in a roomful of people pretending to have a good time and saying, 'Oh, isn't this fun?' when it isn't. That's silly. People say, 'Oh, but you ought to get out—you ought to go to the movies or the theater more often.' Why? I think it's a waste of time, doing things you don't really want to because people thing you ought to."

However, in 1970, Carson met Joanna Holland at a time when his marriage to Joanne was on the rocks, having succumbed to the same combination of selfishness and infidelity that had killed his marriage to Joan. Though he was still married, he was happy to have Joanna become his mistress as long as she under stood the rules. According to one close friend, Carson's attitude toward the woman he was with was, "You're mine. You come when I call. If it's in the middle of the night, whenever. If I ever see your name in the paper, you're through. When I'm through with you, you get in the car and leave, except if I want you to stay overnight. And if I want you to stay overnight, you stay overnight."

Joanna Holland

Though she was a young, beautiful professional model with the world at her feet, these were the rules Joanna agreed to. Over the next two years, Carson would go through a very messy divorce and finally agree to pay Joanne a significant amount of alimony just to be free to marry Joanna. Then, during the party being held on September 30, 1972 to celebrate Carson's 10th anniversary with *The Tonight Show*, he announced that he had married Joanna. Of course, by this time everyone was talking about each of his wives' first names: Joan, Joanne and Joanna. When asked about this, Carson just quipped that it was an easy way to avoid having to buy new monogrammed towels.

Of course, so many short lived marriages elicited a certain amount of speculation, even in

Hollywood, but Carson was sanguine about it: "I couldn't care less what anybody says about me. I live my life, especially my personal life, strictly for myself. I feel that is my right, and anybody who disagrees with that, that's his business. Whatever you do, you're going to be criticized. I feel the one sensible thing you can do is try to live in a way that pleases you. If you don't hurt anybody else, what you do is your own business." All the while, he managed to keep cracking jokes about marriage: "My giving advice on marriage is like the captain of the Titanic giving lessons on navigation."

In 1972, Carson also agreed to move the taping of the show from New York City to Burbank, California, after several years resisting the idea because he preferred life on the East Coast. However, he eventually became disenchanted with the noise and crowds in New York, and unlike California, there were no nearby suburbs where he could live and commute to the studio. Thus, he chose to move to the West Coast with his new wife and the entire *Tonight Show* crew. When asked about his decision, he told reporters, "The main reason is the talent pool. There's not much television in New York anymore. When you do five shows every week for a year, it's a little sticky sometimes to find a large number of lively people in New York." As a result, Carson was soon introducing his show from 'beautiful downtown Burbank."

However, the move out west introduced a new set of problems for the show, and one that the producers could not have initially anticipated came up during the late 1970s. The crew filmed the show at 5:30 each evening for broadcast at 8:30 Pacific time (11:30 Eastern). They would transmit this live show via satellite to New York for editing, but the transmission was usually about two and a half hours long. Knowing that much of the show would be edited out, Carson and the members of the band would often make comments that were not suitable for public consumption, but some individuals began purchasing satellite dishes to catch programs being transmitted through the air. This allowed people to pick up *The Tonight Show* uncensored, and as word spread, people began setting their dishes to catch the often risqué show. As a result, NBC was forced to change to microwave transmissions during the early 1980s, and the studio eventually decided to simply move the editing facilities to Burbank.

Another problem arose in December 1973. Commenting on the many shortages plaguing the country at that time, Carson jokingly said that there was a threat of a severe shortage of toilet paper, but many of his viewers took his predictions seriously and rushed out to stock up on bath tissue. This in turn led to real shortages, and some companies had to ration supplies until they could make more, which created something of a self-fulfilling prophesy. Ultimately, Carson took a few moments from a January broadcast to apologize and clarify his comments.

The 1970s also introduced a new character to the show: Floyd R. Turbo, American. Played by a plaid coat wearing Carson, the character was meant to be "the epitome of the redneck ignoramus. I find the things (characteristics) each week when I go out to do...his gestures at the wrong time, his not knowing where he's supposed to be, his feeble attempts at humor, his talks about things he doesn't quite understand." He was known for such pithy observations as "If God didn't want us to hunt, He wouldn't have given us plaid shirts"; "I only kill in self-defense—what would you do if a rabbit pulled a knife on you?", and "Baseball the way it was meant to be played, on real grass, with no designated hitter and all white guys."

The late 1970s saw *The Tonight Show* win a number of awards, and for four years in a row, from 1976-79, it won a special Emmy for Outstanding Program and Individual Achievement. Carson was especially proud of the acclaim because he recognized the difficulty of maintaining such a high standard on a show that aired each weekday: "…a lot of the time TV is judged by the wrong standards. If Broadway comes up with two first-rate new plays in a season, the critics are delighted. That's a good season. But on TV they expect that every week. It's a very visible medium to jump on. And there's another thing that isn't generally realized. If you're selling hard goods—like soap or dog food—you simply can't afford to put on culture. Exxon, the Bank of America—organizations like that can afford to do it. But they aren't selling hard goods, and that's what the 'Tonight Show' has to do."

Politically, Carson was a liberal, but he also knew the danger of making his personal views known on his show, as he explained to *The New Yorker*, "Now, I think Hustler is tawdry, but I also think that if the First Amendment means what it says, then it protects Flynt as much as anyone else, and that includes the American Nazi movement. As far as I'm concerned, people should be allowed to read and see whatever they like, provided it doesn't injure others. If they want to read pornography until it comes out of their ears, then let them. But if I go on *The Tonight Show* and defend Hustler, the viewers are going to tag me as that guy who's into pornography. And that's going to hurt me as an entertainer, which is what I am."

For all that he enjoyed pushing the boundaries of good taste, Carson never forgot that those boundaries existed, and he was particularly hard on the supposedly avant garde humor of the 1970s: "It always amazes me, the things people regard as comedy in the theater. Any show where the biggest laugh is 'son-of-a-bitch' isn't much comedy in my book. I go to see what I think I'll enjoy. For me to spend three hours in a theater because something is charming just isn't what I want to do."

In 1979, Carson hosted the Academy Award Ceremony in Hollywood for the first time, and he hosted each of the following three years and again in 1984. In order to have more time for this and other extracurricular pursuits, Carson asked that *The Tonight Show* be cut to 60 minutes a show, and he also began using guest hosts even more often, making Joan Rivers his "permanent guest host" from 1983-1986. However, she subsequently left the show for her own talk show, *The Joan Rivers Show*, which aired on Fox opposite Carson's for the next season. Carson considered this a form of betrayal, and the two stopped being friends. Rivers would later recall that Carson wouldn't say a word to her when they bumped into each other, but either way, Jay Leno took over the Monday night slot in 1987.

Joan Rivers was not the only celebrity to have a falling out with Carson. Singer Wayne Newton often appeared on *The Tonight Show*, but during the mid-1980s, Carson began making jokes about him that Newton found offensive. After trying to contact Carson by phone, Newton finally showed up at the studio and demanded to see Carson. According to his recollection,

> "I said to Mr. Carson, I said, I don't know what friend of yours I've killed, I don't know what child of yours I've hurt, I don't know what food I've taken out of your mouth, but these jokes about me will stop and they'll stop now or I will kick your ass.
>
> He started to mumble, and I think he said something like, Wayne, I'm your biggest fan. I said, don't give me that crap. Don't give me that. I am here to straighten out whatever your problem is. And whichever way you want to straighten it out is fine with me.
>
> Johnny Carson was a mean-spirited human being. And there are people that he has hurt that people will never know about. And for some reason at some point, he decided to turn that kind of negative attention toward me. And I refused to have it."

While Johnny Carson was certainly hard to work with and live with, he was a very generous man when it came to good causes. In 1981, Carson established The John W. Carson Foundation to support causes related to the health and well-being of children. He was also very supportive of the financial needs in his hometown of Norfolk, Nebraska, donating much of the money needed to establish the Carson Cancer Center at Faith Regional Health Services and the Johnny Carson Theater at Norfolk Senior High School. He was also a significant contributor to the Elkhorn Valley Museum in Norfolk.

However, during this period, Carson also again found himself in divorce court when Joanna filed for divorce in 1983. Since California is a community property state, she would get 50% of all the assets Carson had gained during their marriage, which was no small issue, because Carson had spent much of that time being the highest paid person on television, making over $4 million a year. As a result, the proceedings dragged out, and the divorce was not finalized until 1985. Two years later Carson married Alexis Maas, and the fourth time turned out to be the charm, as their marriage lasted until Carson's death.

Understandably, this was a very difficult time in Carson's life, and he again fell into the habit of drinking more than he should. In 1982, he was stopped and arrested for driving under the influence of alcohol. His lawyer got the charge dropped to a misdemeanor, and Carson pleaded nolo contendere in return for a reduced sentence of three years' probation. As part of his sentence, Carson was only allowed to drive to and from the studio, and he was not allowed to have another person or even an animal in the car with him while he drove. He also had to take a class in understanding the effect of alcohol on driving.

As he got older, Carson became more and more interested in a hobby he had picked up in high school: astronomy. He owned several telescopes, including the famous Questar telescope, considered the best available at the time, and his star status allowed him to meet and even become friends with the famous astronomer Carl Sagan. In turn, Carson used his show to promote Sagan and his work, often inviting him to appear on *The Tonight Show*. Carson was one of the first celebrities to pick up on Sagan's unique speech pattern when talking about the night sky, and often mocked him by saying "BILLions and BILLions."

Sagan

Carson's other favorite hobby was tennis. He had always been athletic and found tennis to be a great way to keep in shape. When he learned that tennis legend John McEnroe was interested in buying his house in Malibu, he agreed to sell it to him only if he would give him six free tennis lessons. At first, McEnroe must have thought he was kidding, but Carson actually had the agreement written into the sales contract.

Chapter 5: Retirement

"Never continue in a job you don't enjoy. If you're happy in what you're doing, you'll like yourself, you'll have inner peace. And if you have that, along with physical health, you will have had more success than you could possibly have imagined." – Johnny Carson

In 1987, Carson celebrated his 25th year as the host of The Tonight Show. In recognition of this landmark, he received his own coveted Peabody Award from the Grady College of Journalism at the University of Georgia. In honoring him, the selection board observed that he had "become an American institution, a household word, the most widely quoted American…[so they] felt the time had come to recognize the contributions that Johnny has made to television, to humor, and to America."

However, a few years later, Johnny Carson suffered a tragedy that every parent fears most. On June 21, 1991, his youngest son, Richard, was killed in an automobile accident near Cayucos, California. Richard was an avid photographer and may have been trying to take some photographs of the scenic drive when he lost control of his car and drove off a steep hill. When Carson finally returned to work after Richard's death, he paid tribute to his son and his art by showing pictures of both as Stevie Ray Vaughan played "Riviera Paradise" in the background.

It is hard to say just how much Richard's death affected Carson's decision to retire from *The Tonight Show*, but either way, all good things must come to an end at some point. For *The Tonight Show Starring Johnny Carson*, that end came less than a year after Ricky's death on the evening of May 22, 1992. Though he was only 66 years old, Carson was understandably tired of the daily grind. During the opening monologue of his final episode, he told his audience, "If I could magically, somehow, that tape you just saw, make it run backwards. I would like to do the whole thing over again. It's been a hell of a lot of fun. As an entertainer, it has been the great experience of my life, and I cannot imagine finding something in television after I leave tonight that would give me as much joy and pleasure, and such a sense of exhilaration, as this show has given me. It's just hard to explain."

Then, after an hour long retrospective of his 30 years with the program, he closed with: "And so it has come to this: I, uh... am one of the lucky people in the world; I found something I always wanted to do and I have enjoyed every single minute of it. I want to thank the people who've shared this stage with me for thirty years. Mr. Ed McMahon, Mr. Doc Severinsen, and you people watching. I can only tell you that it has been an honor and a privilege to come into your homes all these years and entertain you. And I hope when I find something that I want to do and I think you would like and come back, that you'll be as gracious in inviting me into your home as you have been. I bid you a very heartfelt good night." The show then ended with one final image, a photo taken by Richard Carson himself. The following week, Jay Leno took over the show permanently from Carson.

Many people wondered how well Carson would survive without the stimulation of a daily show to tape; after all, George Axelrod had once observed of Carson, "Socially, he doesn't exist. The reason is that there are no television cameras in living rooms. If human beings had little red lights in the middle of their foreheads, Carson would be the greatest conversationalist on Earth." Even Carson himself left the door open for his return to television with some new show or project, but it would never happen.

As it turned out, Carson would take almost a completely opposite course. In the years following his retirement he was rarely seen on film and almost never sat for an interview. When NBC held their 75th Anniversary celebration, Carson even refused to participate. One of the few television "appearances" he made was when he voiced himself in a 1993 episode of *The Simpsons*, "Krusty Gets Kancelled." Carson also appeared on the TV Special *Bob Hope: The First 90 Years* that year.

Looking back on his career with *The Tonight Show*, Carson later recalled, "I'm often asked, 'What is your favorite moment during the 30 years you hosted [The Tonight Show]?' I really don't have just one. The times I enjoyed the most were the spontaneous, unplanned segments that just happened, like Ed Ames' infamous 'Tomahawk Toss' that produced one of the longest laughs in television history. When these lucky moments happen, you just go with them and enjoy the experience and high of the moment."

In November 1993 Carson called in to *Late Show with David Letterman* and even made a rare television appearance on the show in 1994. On May 13, Letterman announced that his sidekick Larry "Bud" Melman would be delivering the "Top Ten List" as Johnny Carson. Instead, Melman delivered the list badly and then stalked off the stage. Looking down, Letterman deadpanned that Melman had been given the wrong list and asked that the "real" list be used. At that moment, Carson himself came out as the band played "Johnny's Theme." The audience went wild, giving Carson a standing ovation, and the late night legend smiled and waved before asking Letterman if he could sit behind his desk. Letterman stepped aside, and Carson sat there for a short time as the crowd continued to cheer. Carson left the stage a few minutes later without ever reading the famous list, later claiming he had lost his voice due to a bad case of laryngitis. Whether or not this was true is anyone's guess, but Carson would never appear on television again.

Of course, Carson being on Letterman's show at all is a very strange turn of events, considering Letterman was the arch-rival of his replacement, Jay Leno. Just before Carson died, Letterman admitted that Carson would occasionally send him jokes that he would in turn work into his monologue, and upon his death, Letterman would mourn, "It's a sad day for his family and for the country. All of us who came after are pretenders. We will not see the likes of him again. He gave me a shot on his show and in doing so, he gave me a career. A night doesn't go by that I don't ask myself, 'What would Johnny have done?' He has been greatly missed since his retirement."

Although Carson worked hard to stay out of the limelight during his retirement, he still kept busy, primarily with charitable pursuits. In 2004, he donated $5.3 million to the University of

Nebraska Foundation, and the money was earmarked for the Department of Theater Arts at the University's Hixson-Lied College of Fine and Performing Arts. This donation was used to fund the Johnny Carson School of Theater and Film.

Chapter 6: Good Night

"I'd say it was quite important to let people hear the opinions of people like Paul Ehrlich, Carl Sagan, Gore Vidal, Margaret Mead. . . We've also taken an interest in local politics. One year, there were eleven candidates for Mayor of Burbank, and we had to give them all equal time. That was pretty public-spirited. But what's important? I think it's important to show ordinary people doing extraordinary things. Like we once had a Japanese guy from Cleveland who wanted to be a cop but he was too short, so his wife had been hanging him up every night by his heels. And it's important to help people live out their fantasies, like when I pitched to Mickey Mantle on the show, or when I played quarterback for the New York Jets." – Johnny Carson

Carson enjoyed the first few years of his retirement, living quietly at home with Alexis, playing a little tennis, and spending many evenings admiring the night sky. He had all the money and fame anyone could want and seemed content, but unfortunately, his happiness would not last. In the early morning hours of March 19, 1999, Carson woke suddenly in his home in Malibu to squeezing pains in his chest. Alarmed, Alexis called an ambulance and had him transported to the nearest hospital, where doctors diagnosed his complaint as a severe heart attack. Further tests showed multiple blockages in his heart, and within days, Carson had undergone quadruple-bypass surgery to open the blockages and repair as much heart damage as possible.

As the heart attack made clear, Carson's health was so bad due to his lifelong addiction to smoking. He had begun smoking as a young man, and he even smoked on the air during many of his early *Tonight Show* broadcasts. However, he began having problems with his lungs as early as the mid-1970s, and occasionally he even told people, "These things are killing me." Sadly he was right.

As the new millennium dawned, Carson was already developing symptoms of the lung disease emphysema that would eventually kill him. Soon he needed oxygen to help him breathe and regular treatments to try to clear his lungs. In the late summer of 2002, he admitted publicly that his doctors had told him he was dying, but he held on for more than two years. During the first few weeks of 2005, he was hospitalized at Cedars-Sinai Medical Center in West Hollywood in respiratory distress, and this time he would not get out alive, dying in the early morning hours of January 23, 2005. In keeping with the private way in which he preferred to live, there was no public funeral or memorial service. His body was cremated, and his ashes were returned to Alexis.

Of course, no one could stop the world from mourning in its own way. The sitting President of the United States, George W. Bush issued a statement praising Carson's good work both on and off the screen. *The Tonight Show with Jay Leno* hosted a retrospective and brought on many of Carson's closest friends and favorite guests, including Ed McMahon, Don Rickles and Drew Carey. Each took time to share what they remembered best about Carson, in between clips of the man himself giving monologues and harassing guests.

For his part, David Letterman paid tribute to the man who had given him his start by giving a monologue that he later admitted consisted entirely of jokes written by Carson himself. He brought on the former executive producer of *The Tonight Show*, Peter Lassally, as well as Carson's own bandleader, Doc Severinsen. In opening the show, Letterman observed that no matter what was going on in America or around the world, for thirty-years the viewing public had just wanted to be "tucked in by Johnny" at the end of their day. Severinsen closed the show with one of Carson's favorite songs, "Here's That Rainy Day."

Severinsen

When the cable network Comedy Central held its First Annual Comedy Awards Ceremony in 2011, one of the awards it gave out was the Johnny Carson Award. David Letterman was the first recipient of the prize, with Don Rickles winning it the following year.

Even after death, Carson kept on giving. He left $5 million to the University of Nebraska, and a few years later, his estate gave another million to the university to endow the "Johnny Carson

Opportunity Scholarship Fund." However, his biggest contribution was to his own John W. Carson Foundation; upon his death, they received $156 million from his estate, which made the foundation by far the largest charitable organization in Hollywood.

In 2012, PBS aired a two-hour documentary on Carson's life and career. Entitled *Johnny Carson: King of the Late Night*, it featured clips from the show and interviews with many who knew Carson best. One reviewer captured what the show portrayed, and really much of who Carson was, when he said, "If to know Carson was to find him unknowable, there nevertheless seems to be remarkable agreement among observers about who he was off-camera: smart, decent, loyal but also demanding loyalty, a person whose natural shyness was amplified by his Midwest roots…"

Online Resources

Other books about 20th century American history by Charles River Editors

Other books about entertainers by Charles River Editors

Other books about Ed Sullivan on Amazon

Other books about Johnny Carson on Amazon

Bibliography

Harris, Michael. Always On Sunday: An Inside View of Ed Sullivan, the Beatles, Elvis, Sinatra & Ed's Other Guests (2010)

Ilson, Bernie. Sundays with Sullivan: How the Ed Sullivan Show Brought Elvis, the Beatles, and Culture to America (2010)

Maguire, James. Impresario: The Life and Times of Ed Sullivan (2011)

Nachman, Gerald. Right Here on Our Stage Tonight!: Ed Sullivan's America (2009)

Bushkin, Henry (2013). Johnny Carson. Houghton, Mifflin,Harcourt.

Carson, Johnny (1965). Happiness is a Dry Martini. Doubleday and Company.

Carson, Johnny (1967). Misery is a blind date. Doubleday and Company.

Cox, Stephen (2002). Here's Johnny: Thirty Years of Americas Favorite Late Night Entertainer. Cumberland House Publishing.

De Cordova, Fred (1988). Johnny Came Lately. Simon & Schuster.

Ephron, Nora (1968). and now...Here's Johnny!. Avon Books.

Hise, James Van (1992). 40 Years at Night: the Story of the Tonight Show. Movie Publisher Services.

Leamer, Laurence (2005). King of the Night: The Life of Johnny Carson. Avon

McMahon, Ed (2005). Here's Johnny!: My Memories of Johnny Carson, The Tonight Show, and 46 Years of Friendship. Thomas Nelson.

Sweeney, Don (2005). Backstage at the Tonight Show, from Johnny Carson to Jay Leno. Taylor Trade Publishing.

Tennis, Craig (1980). Johnny Tonight: A Behind the Scenes Closeup of Johnny Carson & the Tonight Show. Pocket Books.

Free Books by Charles River Editors

We have brand new titles available for free most days of the week. To see which of our titles are currently free, click on this link.

Discounted Books by Charles River Editors

We have titles at a discount price of just 99 cents everyday. To see which of our titles are currently 99 cents, click on this link.

Made in the USA
Middletown, DE
03 October 2016